Barry Took and Marty Feldman

Round the Horne

with drawings by Hewison

Futura Publications Limited

A Futura Book

First published in Great Britain in 1974
by The Woburn Press

First Futura Publications edition 1975
published in association with
The Woburn Press

ISBN: 0 8600 7247 9

Futura Publications Limited
49 Poland Street, London W1A 2LG

The Publishers acknowledge with thanks
the co-operation of the BBC

Acknowledgements are also due to:
BBC Photograph Library for the
photograph of Douglas Smith; Fraser &
Dunlop Ltd. for the photographs of Betty
Marsden, Hugh Paddick, and Barry Took
and Marty Feldman; Axel Poignant for the
photographs of Kenneth Horne and
Kenneth Williams.

FOREWORD

To Barry Took

Dear Sir or Madman,

As you know, I always like to keep my ear to the ground, which explains the curious crouching position I'm forced to adopt when out strolling and which fact led to that 'incident' involving a Dagenham girl piper and a mirror on the end of a broom handle which rocked all of Crouch End to its very found- ations in the Spring of '67. However, I digress. There, I've admitted it, I do digress. I've told you now inspector and I'm glad, I tell you, glad.

Keeping my ear to the ground I've heard ominous rumblings from that gaggle of swarthy trolls yclept The Woburn Press that they intend to make public some of the whimsical filth we passed off as Round the Horne scripts. I am shocked, as no doubt you are, that this trashy volume may fall into the hands of certain irresponsible and gullible folks like Mary Whitehouse or Pope Muggeridge who may be corrupted by its contents and use it as licence to rip up railway seats, savagely attack rabbits, or bite old age pensioners in the leg, as it so often caused us to do while we were writing this stuff.

I understand that you are assembling this 'book' and will no doubt be recounting some of the background material. I beg you, in the name of all that's holy, to suppress any mention of the 'Bognor scandal' since the lady in question is now trying to start a new life as a wrestling goat sexer in Hamburg and the Archbishop, of course, recovered.

The Goat in Boots had its leg amputated as a result of the party in Kenneth Williams' bicycle shed and left the Balls Pond Road under a cloud no bigger than a man's nose and now earns a precarious living posing for pub signs.

Good luck with your oeuvre. I must get back to my work now. I am, as you may have heard, trying for the world's longest suicide attempt by stuffing live nightingales down my throat until their beaks stick out of my ankles. My best to you, and yours. My second best to them and theirs. The rest to be equally divided among the needy of Saudi Arabia.

Phineas T. Gruntfuttock
née Marty Feldman

CONTENTS

INTRODUCTION

The point about working on Round The Horne was that it was fun.

My strongest memory is of Kenneth Horne wiping tears of laughter from his eyes as Kenneth Williams or one of the other cheery lunatics who made up the cast improvised some brilliant stroke of characterisation. Funnily enough they never altered the script much, the 'ad libs' were more often than not written in, but the characters the cast invented verged on genius.

Because radio is so much a thing of the imagination those characters linger in the mind (in common with Eccles, Bluebottle, the Glums, Mrs Mopp and the rest) long after television characters are forgotten.

Historically, Round The Horne was created at a time, 1964, when most people thought that radio was dead. Its abundant success however proved them wrong. Its predecessor Beyond Our Ken, on which I had worked for forty odd programmes with Eric Merriman, had been more or less contemporary with Take It From Here, Hancock, and The Goons. By the time Marty Feldman and I were asked to write a new series for Kenneth Horne and the gang, those programmes had vanished or transferred to television.

Marty and I had worked mainly in TV creating, among other things, the hugely successful Bootsie and Snudge for Granada, and frankly were not at first interested in a radio show—but the prospect of working with *that* cast and *that* producer (John Simmonds) was, as it were, an offer we couldn't refuse.

Marty and I wrote fifty shows in all, changing the format from time to time as the whim took us, and allowing our imagination to roam freely. When Marty went back to performing, I carried on with Donald Webster and Johnnie Mortimer and Brian Cooke for a further twenty odd shows. Kenneth Horne's death terminated what had been the happiest period of my writing life.

Memories of the show abound. I remember once being en route to the coast stuck in a mile long traffic jam one Sunday lunchtime. I suddenly realised that everyone in that traffic jam was listening to Round The Horne—everybody had their windows open, everybody was laughing—a traffic snarl up suddenly turned into a festival. On another occasion I can remember Marty and I in a Soho sandwich bar listening to the customers heatedly discussing whether Rambling Syd Rumpo's songs were dirty or not.

When the BBC sold the show worldwide, including the USA, we had a lot of fun wondering what the listening millions in the Yemen and Ghana and Atlanta, Georgia would make of such phrases as 'How bona to vada your dolly old eek again', and 'riddle me possetts and griddle me nodes'. There were some criticisms of the show, including the curious complaint that the cast 'put emphasis on certain words', but the BBC Governors liked it and so did millions of listeners. But the people who liked it most were the cast, the production team, the band and the writers—and there's not many shows of which you can say that.

If I had to sum up the success of Round The Horne, I would say that it was the natural link, indeed almost the only link between the golden age of radio comedy (ITMA, Goons) and the new wave (Monty Python et al.). It never looked down on its audience, it was never snobbish and it was the perfect setting for that best of men—Kenneth Horne.

BARRY TOOK

THE CAST

Kenneth Horne first went 'on the Air' in Britain in 1940 when, as a member of the R.A.F., he was instructed by his superior officer to organise a broadcast. He ended the war with the rank of Wing Commander and went on to combine a successful career in British industry – he had read economics at Cambridge – with his radio and television work. He had a long and fruitful association with Richard Murdoch which resulted in the popular wartime and post-war radio show 'Much Binding in the Marsh'. In 1958, the year 'Beyond Our Ken' burst upon an unsuspecting public, Kenneth Horne decided to retire from industry, and devoted all his time to broadcasting until his death in 1969.

Born in London, **Kenneth Williams** was educated both in London and abroad, and served in the Army in the Far East. A star of stage, screen, and radio who first came to prominence in Anouilh's 'The Lark', he has worked extensively in revue (Share My Lettuce', 'Pieces of Eight', etc.), appeared in many 'Carry On' films, and had his own television show.

Betty Marsden was born in Liverpool, studied at the Italian Conti Stage School, and toured for E.N.S.A. during the war. An accomplished actress in both farce and straight theatre, her career has included work in radio and television as well as many stage performances. Her last West End appearance was in 'The Prime of Miss Jean Brodie'.

Born in Hoddesdon, Hertfordshire, **Hugh Paddick** began his professional life in law, but soon found that he preferred a theatre audience to a crowded court room. As well as his wide range of work in radio and television he has been a frequent performer on the West End stage, including three and a half years as Colonel Pickering in the Drury Lane production of 'My Fair Lady'.

Since his first professional appearance as an impressionist in concert party in 1955, **Bill Pertwee** has been steadily engaged in work for radio, television, stage, and film. He is now firmly established as the Air Raid Warden in 'Dad's Army', and has just begun a new radio series, 'The Worst Show on the Wireless'.

Douglas Smith joined the European Service of the BBC in 1946, and went on to be an announcer and newsreader for the Home Service and television. In addition to his participation in 'Beyond Our Ken' and 'Round the Horne', he pursued his interest in works for narrator and music until his death in 1972.

Tony Hayes (*left*) studied art, and **Jimmy Fraser** engineering, before they each dropped out to become dance band guitarists. They met and formed their group in the 'fifties, and worked together in variety, clubs, TV, and radio until 1967. Jimmy now follows a solo career in the U.S., while Tony continues with his present group, The Skylarks.

THE MAIN CHARACTERS

JULIAN AND SANDY

Hugh   Kenneth
Paddick   Williams

Always to be found where the effete meet,
these two ex-chorus boys are game for
anything.
From working as part time domestics while
'resting' they progressed to running almost
every trendy activity going from fox hunting
in Carnaby Street to the gents outfitting
department of MI5. They live in Chelsea with
their friend Gordon, a former attendant at the
local Slipper baths.
Julian is possibly the more sensitive of the
two but nobody likes to go near enough to
find out.
Clubs: The Marine Commando, Paddington.
       The Sheep's Eye, Tangiers.
Hobbies: You must be joking!

RAMBLING SYD RUMPO

Kenneth Williams

An itinerate folk singer whose ganderbag
always contains at least one new ditty to
screeve your cordwangle and bring moulies to
your possett. As Rambling Syd himself says
'What care I for the city life—all I want is the
sky for my coverlet and a bosky turve for my
pillow. My only viand's hedgehog pâté washed
down with a simple unpretentious paraffin
rosé'. Rambling Syd Rumpo is one of the last
of the breed of wandering minstrels who are
fast dying out—thank heavens.

DAME CELIA MOLESTRANGLER

Betty Marsden

and

BINKIE HUCKABACK

Hugh Paddick

as

FIONA AND CHARLES

What would London's West End Theatre be
without these ineffable thespians? How can
one describe them without invoking the law
of libel? They're earthquakingly, mind
bendingly, stomach turningly, heart
stoppingly, knee tremblingly awful, but
somehow wonderfully, terribly real and yet
somehow—unreal.

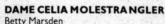

DAPHNE WHITETHIGH

Betty Marsden

A hoarse-voiced fashion plater and sometime
cookery expert whose advice on the placing of
the bosom or the way to prepare Hippo in its
shell is an absolute must for all those trendy
moderns who want to look and feel frightful.

SEAMUS ANDROID

Bill Pertwee

An unskilled television labourer whose gift of
the blarney and wistful Irish charm could
empty any theatre in three minutes.

CHOU EN GINSBERG M.A. (Failed)
Kenneth Williams

Fiendish Japanese mastermind. His reason
was turned when he failed an audition as a
BBC announcer on account of being too tall.
Has sworn to take his revenge on Western
Civilisation and from all the evidence is doing
it extremely effectively.

LOTUS BLOSSOM
Hugh Paddick

Concubine to Chou En Ginsberg. Brings solace
to the mastermind and acts as a decoy to
unwary occidentals. Her many
accomplishments include singing, watercolour
painting, engraving the thoughts of Confucius
on grains of rice, and playing the trombone.
She is, in the words of her master, 'as
common as muck.'

'DENTURES'
Hugh Paddick

A man with ill fitting false teeth, and you
can't say fairer than that.

LADY BEATRICE COUNTERBLAST (NEE CLISSOLD)
Betty Marsden

Much married, much divorced, ex-gaiety
girl who now lives in seclusion at Chattering
Parva, served occasionally by her faithful
octogenarian butler, Spasm. Her anecdotes of
past marriages combine the lurid with the
turgid as the narrative flashes back on leaden
wings to the turn of the century and the
exploits of the young Bea Clissold.

SPASM
Kenneth Williams

Lady Counterblast's butler. 'Get thee away
from this doomed pile' croaks the old loony.
'We be doomed—we all be doomed'. Be he
man or be he ghastly manifestation? It's a
question that's been asked 'many many
times'—but only with the light on.

J. PEASEMOULD GRUNTFUTTOCK
Kenneth Williams

The "walking slum", sometime King of
Peasemoldia, a small derelict area off the
Balls Pond Road. Would-be TV executive and
persistent letter writer. His habits and
behaviour may seem a trifle eccentric to the
outsider but to anyone who knows him they
are downright inscrutable. J. Peasemold
Gruntfuttock is guided by 'voices' and one
can only hope that one day they'll guide him
into the Grand Union Canal. He married
beneath him—which gives you some idea of
what his wife, Buttercup (Betty Marsden)
must be like. All in all, not a couple one would
wish to meet on a dark night or indeed at
any time.

THE BACKROOM BOYS OF THE BBC

Somewhere between boiler house and
boardroom, between Portland Place and
Wood Lane lurk the eccentric arbiters of
taste and discretion that have made the BBC
an enigma in its own lifetime. They are, of
course, entirely imaginary. (Ironic laughter).

DOBBIROIDS

The Magic Horse Rejuvenator, not a character
but an amalgam of all quack medicines.
Absolutely guaranteed to ease tired hooves
and take the flock off the wallpaper.
Dobbiroids and its by-products are designed
to give horses a new lease of life—sort of
instant Mark Philips one could say.
Couldn't one?

11

CAMP CHAT

A glossary of words and phrases used by Julian and Sandy and their (printable) meanings.

Palare	=	Talk (Romany)
Bona	=	Good
Vada	=	Look
Omi	=	Man
Palone	=	Woman
Omipaloni	=	Homosexual
Riah	=	Hair
Lallies	=	Legs
Dolly	=	Nice/pleasant
Eek	=	Face
Naph	=	Bad
Nante	=	None/nothing
Lucoddy	=	Body
Fantabulosa	=	Excellent
Troll	=	Walk
Lattie	=	House

Most of the words are of gypsy origin or fairground and circus slang now used by actors and dancers in other branches of the theatre. Some words are Kenneth Williams' and Hugh Paddick's own natural form of expression!

THE RAMBLING SYD RUMPO SONG BOOK

Unlike Julian and Sandy's slang, which if
bizarre is authentic, all the strange words
used by Rambling Syd were invented for
the character. They mean nothing but
sound as if they might.

(First broadcast 10th June 1965)

RAMBLING SYD: (SPOKEN) **This song tells the story of a country lass who sings to her soldier sweetheart—'Oh soldier, soldier when shall we be wed? For I'm tired of the single life and besides, the neighbours are starting to talk and I can't keep telling 'em you've come to read the gas meter.' And he answers, 'Oh winsome maid, oh pretty maid, fain would I make thee my wife-o, but we cannot be wed for I have no boots to put on.' So she goes and buys him a pair of fine boots, and then she sings, 'Oh soldier, soldier when shall we be wed?' And he sings, 'Fain would I make thee my wife-o but I have no trousis to put on.' So she gets him a pair of fine trousis and then she sings 'Soldier, soldier when shall we be wed?' And he sings—'Hang on a minute, I can't get these fine trousis on over my boots, and anyway I cannot marry thee as I have no belt.' So she gives him one, and he goes, and as he runs off he sings this stirring martial strain—**

(No tune known to man)

RAMBLING SYD: (SINGS)
Fare thee well my apple-cheeked Betty-o,
Fare thee well, fare thee well.
For I'm off to fight my country foes
So dry your eyes and wipe your nose
Nose-o, nose-o.
For Billy has gone to the wars-o
A rub a-dub dub, for the sabres clash
With a musket, fife and drum-a-diddle eye do,
With my billycock hat on my billycock head
For I'm off to be a dragono-oooooooooooh!

(First broadcast 16th January 1967)

To tune similar to 'Waltzing Matilda'

RAMBLING SYD: (SINGS)
Once long ago in the shade of a goolie bush, ...
Toasting his splod by the faggots gleam,
Rested a gander man nobbling his woggle iron
And stuffing a sheep in the Old Mill Stream.
Then up came the troopers and
    hung him by the billabong,
They twisted his woggle irons one two three –
(*minor*) Now his ghost sits and moans
As it grunges in his gander can –
Who'll come a woggling his jumbuck with me ...
Oh!

RAMBLING SYD: (SPOKEN) **Now my dearios, I'll tether my nadgers to a grouting pole for the old grey mare is grunging in the meadow. Well, better there than here—It makes so much work for the char. Tis about a fabled horse, the Somerset Nog—so called because it's a cross between a nag and a dog. Half Suffolk Punch and half Dachshund. It gets very foggy on the moors. Anyway, the Nog is a strange looking creature—three-hands high and eighteen-foot long. They're not pretty to look at—but the rhubarb in that part of the world be magnificent.**
My song tells of a man who wants to go to the great fair at Ganderpoke Bog—so he asks the farmer for a loan of the Nog, so he can take all his friends with him, and it proceeds in this fashion.

To the tune of 'Widdecombe Fair'

RAMBLING SYD: (SINGS)
Reg Pubes, Reg Pubes
Lend me your great Nog,
Rollock me fussett
and griddle me nodes.
For I want to go-o
to Ganderpoke Bog, with –
Len Possett, Tim Screevy,
the Reverend Phipps,
Peg Leg Loombucket,
Solly Levy, Ginger Epstein,
Able Seaman Truefitt,
Scotch Lil,
Messrs. Cattermole, Mousehabit,
Neapthigh and Trusspot, solicitors
and Commissioners for Oaths,
Father Thunderghast, Fat Alice,
Con Mahoney, Yeti Rosencrantz,
Foo Tong Robinson and Uncle Ted Willis an' all–
and Uncle Ted Willis and all.

(SPOKEN) So they all get on—except **Fat Alice**, who don't get on with anybody, and off they go, but sad to relate—the horse snaps in two and expires—but they do say as how its ghost walks abroad—in two halves, and if you be passing Ganderpoke Bog at midnight they say you can hear the two ghostly halves of the Nog singing in duet . . .

RAMBLING SYD: (SINGS)
Reg Pubes, Reg Pubes
you lent your great Nog –
Rollock me fussett
and grindle me nodes.
And now my remains are in
Ganderpoke Bog – with
(*as quickly as possible*)
Len Possett, Tim Screevy,
the Reverend Phipps,
Peg Leg Loombucket,
Solly Levy, Ginger Epstein,
Able Seaman Truefitt,
Scotch Lil,
Messrs. Cattermole, Mousehabit,
Neapthigh and Trusspot, solicitors
and Commissioners for Oaths,
Father Thunderghast, Fat Alice,
Con Mahoney, Yeti Rosencrantz,
Foo Tong Robinson and Uncle Ted Willis an' all –
And Uncle Ted Willis and all.

(First broadcast 23rd January 1967)

No tune exists for this masterpiece of ineptitude!

RAMBLING SYD: (SINGS)
Twas on the good ship Habbakuk
And I a mid ship mite,
When four days out of Liverpool
A mermaid did I sight.

Singing fare ye well my Betty O
Fare ye well I say.
Fare ye well my pretty young maid
My futtocks be bound away.

(SPOKEN) **Then the mermaid sings to him in wheedling tones—**

(SINGS SEXILY) Come marry me my pretty lad
And live beneath the billow.
A coral reef shall be our bed
An octopus our pillow.

(SINGS IN SYD'S OWN VOICE)
Singing Fare thee well my Mary O
Fare thee well to you.
Fare thee well my pretty young lass,
My futtocks be rusted through.

(SPOKEN) **Seduced by the siren's voice and the fact that he can only see the top half of her sticking up out of the waves, the foolish sailor lad leaps over the side and drowns, and as he goes down for the third time he sings—**

Fare thee well my Sally O,
Fare thee well sweatheart.
I am no use to you my love,
My futtocks have come apart –
Oh!

(First broadcast 13th February 1967)

To the tune of 'Foggy Foggy Dew'

RAMBLING SYD: (SINGS)
When I was a young man
I nadgered my snod
as I nurked at the wogglers trade.
When suddenly I thought
while trussing up my groats,
I'd whirdle with a fair young maid.
We whirdled through the summer time
until the winter came,
and the only thing that I ever did wrong
was to tell her my foggy foggy name.

Now I am married
and I've put away my snod
and my son's at the woggler's trade.
Though I still think
as I'm trussing up my groats
of whirdling with a fair young maid.
I'd whirdle her in the winter time
I'd whirdle her for dear life –
But the only only thing that I'd have to do
Is to keep it from the foggy foggy wife – Oh!

To the tune of 'Clementine'

RAMBLING SYD: (SINGS)
Joe he was a young cordwangler,
Monging greebles did he go,
And he loved a bogler's daughter
By the name of Chiswick Flo.

Vain she was and like a grusset,
Though her ganderparts were fine –
But she sneered at his cordwangle
As it hung upon the line.

So he stole a wogglers moulie,
For to make a wedding ring –
But the Bow Street Runners caught him
And the judge said he will swing.

Oh they hung him by the postern,
Nailed his moulie to the fence –
For to warn all young cordwanglers
That it was a grave offence.

There's a moral to this story
Though your cordwangle be poor –
Keep your hands off others moulies,
For it is against the law. Oh!

(First broadcast 26th February 1967)

RAMBLING SYD: (SPOKEN) **This is a taddle gropers dance, sung by the villagers of Musgrove Parva and it heralds the coming of the oak apple fairy or sanitary inspector, as he is known. The taddle gropers grope round taddling each other while the turve maiden merrily whirdles her splod. They dance to a roundelay that goes after this fashion:**

He sings to an approximation of 'Here we go
Round the Mulberry Bush'

RAMBLING SYD: (SINGS)
There's cordwangles in my possett bag,
What shall I do my May O –
And I can't woggle my artifacts
What shall I do my Darling.

(SPOKEN) **So the turve maiden sings back:**

RAMBLING SYD: (SINGS)
Stove it with a gander hook
That's what to do my Billy O –
Then you can woggle your artifacts
As good as new my darling.

(SPOKEN) **So he stoves it with a gander hook but it don't do no good as a stoat's nibbled the end off and he's forgot to put anti-freeze in so plaintively he sings to her:**

(SINGS) I stoved it in with a gander hook
That's what I've done me Mary O –
But now I've nadgered my artifacts
What shall I do my darling?

(SPOKEN) **So she tells him what to do with his artifacts and he does it—and they dance off woggling and groping their taddles.**

To tune of 'Ye Banks and Braes'

RAMBLING SYD: (SINGS)
Ye nurgs and bogles of Bonnie Glen Postule,
Oft have I greebled amongst your trees,
And whirdled my lassie among your nettles,
Swore my devotion – and stung both my knees.

We bogled and grundled
And grundled and bogled.
I grotted my muckles
For bonnie wee Joan.
But now she's run off with
A plumber from Sidcup,
So I lurk in the forest
And whirdle alone – O.

(First broadcast 20th March 1967)

To tune of 'Lincolnshire Poacher'

RAMBLING SYD: (SINGS)
When I was a clencher's bogle man
In famous Lincoln Town,
I often clenched my bogling fork
For less than half-a-crown.
And I would joggle and nurk my boys
As I shall quickly tell,
Oh tis my delight on a shining night
And a foggy night as well.

Oh once I took my moulies
And I set them in a snare.
Twas then I spied a scropers man
A'whirdling a hare.
But I was not afeared my boys
Of that there is no doubt.
Oh tis my delight on a shining night
When the coppers aren't about.

Although I'm over eighty now
My bogles still I clench.
And I will flutter my artifacts
At any passing wench.
I've tickled many a screebling nut
As on my way I go.
Oh tis my delight on a shining night
At 5op a throw – oooooh!

(First broadcast 24th April 1967)

RAMBLING SYD: (SPOKEN) **Here now is an eerie song, so spine chilling that it'll make the bogles on your posset stand on end. It's the story of a bold highwayman called the Black Grunger of Hounslow, and his exploits—**

To tune of 'Too Ra Lae Aye'

RAMBLING SYD: (SINGS)
Oh list while I sing of a highwayman bold
His feats were remarkable, so we are told.
He'd whirdle the ladies and scrope all the men –
Then he'd straddle his nadger and ride off again.
Singing fiddle me grummits
And scrumple me floot.

They caught him and hung him from
   Old Tyburn Tree,
But e'er the noad screevelled his gurka, quoth he:
'If I had my time to live over again,
I'd scrope all the ladies and whirdle the men.'
Singing fiddle me grummits
And scrumple me floot.

(SPOKEN) **However—they strung him and his horse up, and they do say as how his ghost rides abroad even to this day haunting the place where he once straddled his nadger so gaily. Only unfortunately they've built a supermarket on the site, and on early closing day his wraith can be seen a'galloping along the bacon counter and manifesting itself behind the crystallised fruits. And as he gallops he sings:**

(SINGS SLOWLY)

My tale is ended, my song is sung,
As me and my horse we have both been well hung.
And as I'm a phantom my only recourse
Is to scrope by myself and to whirdle my horse.
Singing fiddle me grummits
And scrumple me (*sepulchral tones*) –
Flooooot!

(First broadcast 8th May 1967)

RAMBLING SYD: (SPOKEN) **And now in more lighthearted vein a pewter wogglers bangling song. After a hard day in the grunge foundry hammering their artifacts the jolly grunge men repair to the local hostelry of fumble shop—and charge their thunder jugs with the foaming nut brown meths. And then they link nadgers and let forth this stirring refrain as follows:**

To tune of 'Come Landlord Fill The Flowing Bowl'

RAMBLING SYD: (SINGS)
Come fellows raise your fumble jugs
    until your cringe is plunging.
Come raise aloft your nut brown grott
    for soon we'll all be munging—
For tonight I'll drain the possett dry,
Every man shall do the same as I—
If he don't I'll whirdle in his eye,
Tomorrow we'll be grunging – ooooh!

(First broadcast 14th June 1967)

RAMBLING SYD: (SPOKEN) **Now let us all burst forth together—so grundle your parts and away we go . . .**

To tune of 'Green Grow The Rushes O'

RAMBLING SYD: (SINGS)
I'll sing you one-oh!
Green grow my nadgers oh.

CHORUS:
What is your one-oh?

RAMBLING SYD:
One's the grunge upon my splod
Masking my cordwangle.
I'll sing you two-oh!
Green grow my nadgers oh.

CHORUS:
What is your two-oh?

RAMBLING SYD:
Two are my looming thrums—
See how they jangle,
One's the grunge upon my splod
Masking my cordwangle.
I'll sing you three-oh!
Green grow my nadgers oh.

CHORUS:
What are your three-oh?

RAMBLING SYD:
Three are the times
I've lunged my groats,
Two are my looming thrums—
See how they jangle,
One's the grungle upon my splod
Masking my cordwangle.
I'll sing you four-oh!
Green grow my nadgers oh.

CHORUS:
What are your four-oh?

RAMBLING SYD:
Four for my whirdlers bent – oh,
Three are the times
I've lunged my groats,
Two are my looming thrums—
See how they jangle,
One's the grunge upon my splod
Masking my cordwangle.
I'll sing you five – oh!
Green grow my nadgers oh.

CHORUS:
What are your five-oh?

RAMBLING SYD:
Five are the wogglers
up my spong,
Four for my whirdlers bent – oh,
Three are the times
I've lunged my groats,
Two are my looming thrums—
See how they jangle.

CHORUS:
One's the grunge upon my splod—

RAMBLING SYD:
It's ruined my cordwangle!

(First broadcast 22nd May 1967)

RAMBLING SYD: (SPOKEN) **Now hoist up your artifacts and keel haul your dandos because it's time now for a rollicking sea shanty. So nurk your throbbers and away we go.**

To tune of 'What Shall We Do With The Drunken Sailor'

RAMBLING SYD: (SINGS)
What shall we do with the drunken nurker,
What shall we do with the drunken nurker,
What shall be do with the drunken nurker,
He's bending his cordwangle.

Hit him in the nadgers with the bosun's plunger,
Slap him on the grummitt with a wrought iron
                         lunger,
Cuff him in the moulies with the Captain's
                         grunger—

Till his bodgers dangle.

Heave ho and up she rises,
Heave ho and up she rises,
Heave ho and up she rises (*pause*) Oh!
He's broken his cordwangle.

THE SCRIPTS

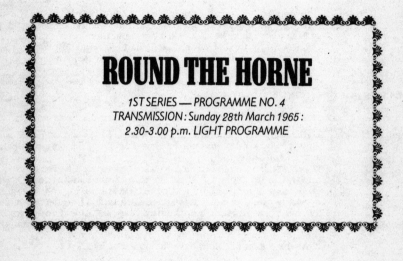

ROUND THE HORNE

1ST SERIES — PROGRAMME NO. 4
TRANSMISSION: Sunday 28th March 1965:
2.30-3.00 p.m. LIGHT PROGRAMME

Douglas Smith	Here are details of some of tonight's programmes.
Bill Pertwee	At eight o'clock there will be a radio history of the Vatican entitled 'Pick of the Popes'.
Hugh Paddick	At ten o'clock Lew Grade will be in the studio giving an excerpt from his autobiography, which is called 'My Life Already'.
Douglas Smith	But meanwhile, for those of you who are more easily pleased, here is thirty minutes of star-studded rubbish as Kenneth Horne takes you 'Round the Horne'.
ORCHESTRA	SIGNATURE TUNE
Douglas Smith	The story so far — last week we left swarthy, bearded Betty Marsden and dusky tigress Hugh Paddick trapped in the Vienna sewers. Suddenly a grating above their heads creaked open and there, silhouetted against the sky, stood a figure that was half man, half beast and half-cut. It opened its yawning maw as it gibbered the words that turned her blood to ice . . .
Kenneth Horne	This is Kenneth Horne.
ORCHESTRA	MUSIC
	(applause)
Kenneth Horne	Hello and welcome to 'Round The Horne'. That was Douglas Smith, who appeared by kind permission of the Alice Tring School of Embalming and Social Club. Now, first, here are the answers to last week's quiz. The answer to question one was in three parts — the three thirty from Paddington, the wheel tapper's daughter, and not while the train is standing in the station. The answer to question two was four-and-six a yard. The other answers were — a henna rinse, Bagshot, a duck billed platypus, Lionel and Joyce Blair or Sammy Davis junior, whichever is the longest, and not, as so many of you thought, a device for opening a malacca walking-stick. Now these days I seldom have the opportunity . . .
Kenneth Williams	(old) Poor old devil, it's a shame.
Hugh Paddick	(old) Don't laugh at him, he might turn nasty.
Kenneth Horne	As I was saying — I seldom have the opportunity . . .
Betty Marsden	(old) Poke him with a stick — see if he moves . . .
Bill Pertwee	(old) Shall I pour a bucket of water over him?
Kenneth Williams	(old) No. Leave him. He'll go away of his own accord.
Kenneth Horne	Doesn't look as if I'm going to get the opportunity today. Anyway — I wanted to mention one of the forgotten men of British Science — Robert 'Capability' Lackwind. The man who gave the world Toad in the Hole.
Hugh Paddick	He can have it back any time.
Kenneth Horne	Capability Lackwind first saw the light of day in September 1832 — when he was forty-five years of age — having spent a secluded life locked in a broom cupboard in Worthing. Before Lackwind's patent Toad in the Hole burst upon an astonished world, there had, of course, been other toads and other holes. There was the Wookey Hole, the coal hole and, of course, the Black Hole of Calcutta, which was claimed to have been

invented by a Mr Ram Singh of Rotherhithe. Nobody believed him because he used to claim all sorts of things, including that he was heir apparent to the throne of Lapland, and even on one occasion that he was Lily Langtry — a claim quickly discredited by a police doctor and Edward the Seventh.

Kenneth Williams	Hurry up — the pubs will be closed . . .
Kenneth Horne	Anyway — holes there were in plenty, but not a toad as far as the eye could see. Capability experimented with all kinds of crude toads, but people scoffed. 'Look at his crude toad' they sneered. 'It's a mockery', but he persevered with true British grit — and in 1862 he produced the first gritty British sausage — or Lackwind's Folly as it was known. A race was arranged between Capability's great sausage and a racehorse. The racehorse won and the giant sausage was buried in State, where it attracted tourists from all over — not to mention the flies. Lackwind passed away soon after, when he fell into a vat of pudding mixture and was found battered to death. To say this led to the War of Jenkins' Ear, is not only a matter of conjecture but absolute nonsense. If you don't believe me — ask Jenkins. You'll have to shout, of course — he's only got one ear.
Kenneth Williams	You finished?
Kenneth Horne	Yes.
Kenneth Williams	Good. I thought we were going to be stuck here all night.
Kenneth Horne	I'm sorry.
Kenneth Williams	It's not for me. It's Hugh Paddick. He gets bitter if he's kept hanging about.
Hugh Paddick	No, it's not that. It's just that I took these tablets just before the show and they work in about twenty minutes, so you see if we're not off the air — well, be it upon your own head . . .
Kenneth Horne	Right. I'll bear that in mind. Now continuing our series — the backroom boys of the BBC, we swing the spotlight onto that much abused but nevertheless essential department, the BBC censors, whose job it is to force out hidden dirt — Wherever there is Honi Soit, there you'll find them Mal y pense-ing. Come with us now, down the Corridors of Power to a small back room in Broadcasting House — where the censors are in session . . .
OMNES	AD LIB CHATTER
F/X	**RAP OF GAVEL ON TABLE**
SIR ARNOLD (Kenneth Williams)	Alright gentlemen, simmer down. There's too much filth going out on the air — it's our job to stop it. Only this morning I heard a reference to a lady's ankle —
OMNES	Depravity! Lewdness! It's Sodom and Gomorrah all over again.
SIR CLIVE (Bill Pertwee)	Where's it going to end, that's what I ask? Yesterday Mrs Dale said she had a ladder in her stocking. Where is it leading to?
LADY BRINK (Betty Marsden)	What about the suggestive titles of programmes?
SIR ARNOLD	Suggestive? (*eagerly*) What? What? What? What? (*collecting himself*) Er — ahem — I mean — er, could you give us an example?

LADY BRINK	Have a Go with Wilfred Pickles. What's the implication of that?
SIR EDWIN (Hugh Paddick)	Well, I don't see the harm in saying Have A Go. I mean, that's not going to corrupt the listeners. Anybody who listens to Have A Go is beyond corruption.
LADY BRINK	It's not that. It's Pickles. With its suggestion of vinegar — and as everyone knows, vinegar is alcoholic — and we know what alcohol leads to.
SIR ARNOLD	(*getting worked up*) Yes — sister! Screaming and carrying on and tearing their clothes off and cursing and fighting and debauchery and tearing their clothes off — (*pause and then calmly*) At least that's what always happens in my case.
SIR CLIVE	Make the fella change his name from Pickles to something health-giving, like grated carrots, good for the eyes.
SIR EDWIN	I take it then that the programme will henceforth be referred to as Have A Go with a Grated Carrot?
LADY BRINK	Yes. There's nothing ambiguous about that. Then I think we ought to do something about Take Your Partners — Gentlemen — who are they fooling — Take Your Partners for what?
SIR EDWIN	Well, surely it's just Old Tyme dancing, isn't it?
SIR ARNOLD	(*feverish*) Aha — dancing — with each other — holding each other close, their hot breath on each other's necks — the proximity of warm flesh through the bombazine — their knees touching — the women with their rouged cheeks and carmined lips — the soft swell of their (*pants*) Oh, oh, oh, Oooooh!
SIR CLIVE	Quick somebody — a damp sponge on the back of his neck.
SIR ARNOLD	Ah, that's better. Now what else have we got?
SIR CLIVE	A programme called Five to Ten ...
SIR ARNOLD	A suggestion of betting. Strike it out.
	(*from here on the scene builds like a revivalist meeting*)
SIR CLIVE	(*shouts*) Let it be stricken!
LADY BRINK	(*shouts*) Out with it, out with it!
SIR ARNOLD	Yes — let it be cast out brothers — for is it not sinful? And is it not written that we shall go forth and scourge the fleshpots of the BBC with whips and scorpions?
SIR CLIVE	(*shouts*) Yea! Hellfire and brimstone shall be their lot! Yea and we shall whip the soles of their feet! Yea, and they shall be cast down even unto the pit!
SIR ARNOLD	(*hysterical*) For are we not all sinners? Yea, I too have erred. Yea, and got caught at it, but I pleaded the headaches!
LADY BRINK	(*screams*) Give your testimony Brother Arnold ...
OMNES	Yea! He is possessed! Cast out the demon, brother!
SIR ARNOLD	I have sinned ...

F/X	**RATTLE OF TAMBOURINE**
SIR ARNOLD	. . . I have been wicked!
F/X	**RATTLE OF TAMBOURINE**
SIR ARNOLD	. . . I did wallow in the fleshpots and did consort with painted women, publicans and did descend even unto entertaining lewd thoughts regarding Ena Sharples' knees.
F/X	**RATTLE OF TAMBOURINE**
OMNES	He has found the path! He has seen the light! Hallelujah brother! Hallelujah!
ORCHESTRA	**'COME AND JOIN US' (SMALL STREET BAND)**
OMNES	AD LIB REVIVAL TYPE SHOUTS
ORCHESTRA	**MUSIC TO A CLIMAX**
	(applause)
Kenneth Horne	That was the BBC Censorship Department, about whom I would like to say — but I can't because it was censored. Now — Trends.
ORCHESTRA	**MUSIC**
Kenneth Horne	This is the part of the show designed for trendy young moderns — the people who are not only but also, and indeed, scarcely. First, fashion.
DAPHNE WHITETHIGH (Betty Marsden)	Trouser-suits are out!
Kenneth Horne	Blast! I've just bought myself one.
DAPHNE WHITETHIGH	But don't throw away that silk Dior creation you bought last year . . .
Hugh Paddick	*(gruff)* There I told you not to throw it away Alf.
Bill Pertwee	*(gruff)* Well, I had to, didn't I? I had to have room to hang up me Balenciagas.
Kenneth Horne	Now, trends in the home. Domestic help is becoming increasingly hard to find. When my au pair went back to Mongolia, frankly I was at a loss. For a time I employed a local woman to come in twice a week to smash the crockery and block up the drains — all the little household things I didn't have time to do myself. But one can't combine an active public life with charring work, and so, when Barbara Cartland . . . gave in her notice, I got on to Rentachap — that's a firm that specialises in hiring out male domestics — you know the sort of thing — out of work actors, filling in between engagements. Anyway, I rang them up and the next morning . . .
F/X	**CHIMES DOORBELL. DOOR OPENS.**
JULIAN (Hugh Paddick)	Hello. We're from Rentachap. I'm Julian and this is my friend, Sandy.
SANDY (Kenneth Williams)	We've come to do for you — *(whispers)* That's never Kenneth Horne.
JULIAN	*(whispers)* It is — it is.

SANDY	(*whispers*) He's quite old isn't he? I wonder if they're his own teeth?
JULIAN	(*whispers*) Ask him.
SANDY	(*whispers*) I don't like to.
Kenneth Horne	Look, have you just popped round to make comments on my personal appearance or are you going to do the housework?
JULIAN	We're seven-and-six an hour you know. Did Miss Brahms at the agency warn you?
Kenneth Horne	Yes, we agreed terms. Quick come in before the neighbours see you. Now, are you experienced in this sort of work?
JULIAN	Well, not exactly — you see we're filling in between engagements — we do commercials mostly — you may have seen us on the telly — you know that ad where she's got it only no-one'll tell her — only someone does, then she has a bath —
Kenneth Horne	Yes.
JULIAN	Well — she gets me dragged up as a rugby full back.
SANDY	And I'm in the one where I'm alone in a room with this beautiful girl and we put out the lights and test chocolates.
Kenneth Horne	I'm not altogether surprised. Now, let me show you what I want doing. This is the living room.
SANDY	Oh ducky, it's pure Rattigan — with a touch of Messel round the Dado.
Kenneth Horne	And through here's the kitchen.
JULIAN	It's a bit Arnold Wesker isn't it? No, I'm afraid not. Kitchen sink isn't us — heartette — we're more drawing-room comedy — or bedroom farce.
Kenneth Horne	Well, do the best you can — here's the dishcloths.
SANDY	Ugh! Green and yellow — we can't be doing with that.
Kenneth Horne	What's the matter with green and yellow dishcloths?
JULIAN	Well see for yourself treash. We're wearing blue — doesn't match at all. No, anyway, we couldn't wash up in here — all the dishes are dirty —
Kenneth Horne	Well, I'm sorry, I'd have washed them up if I'd known.
SANDY	It's the grease, you see — it turns his stomach over. Some people can cope, darling heart, but whenever Julian is confronted with greasy dishes, he bursts into tears.
Kenneth Horne	Well, I wouldn't want to upset him. Perhaps you'd better start on the living room.
JULIAN	Oh yes, that's much more us — Oh look Sandy — a parquet floor — bona! I wish I'd known — I'd have brought me tap-shoes.
Kenneth Horne	If it's all the same to you — I don't want you to dance on it. I want you to polish it.
JULIAN	I'm not going down on my hands and knees — I shall bag me Levis.
Kenneth Horne	Well, dust something then — there, the piano ...

SANDY	Oh, a piano, heartette.
PIANO	**ARPEGGIO**
	PIANO PLAYS ACCOMPANIMENT (VERY DATED) TO 'AIN'T SHE SWEET'
	JULIAN AND SANDY SING — WITH APPROPRIATE VO-DE-O-DO's
Kenneth Horne	Stop it, stop it —
	PIANO GOES INTO STOP CHORUS
F/X	**TAP DANCING ON WOODEN SURFACE**
Kenneth Horne	Stop dancing on my piano. Oi! Bojangles!
	(music stops abruptly)
F/X	**CLANG OF PIANO LID BEING SLAMMED DOWN**
JULIAN	Well really — that's a nice way to treat an artiste I must say! Bring us here under false pretences — treat us like drudges . . .
SANDY	Don't Julian, don't get yourself worked up. If you frown you'll get crow's feet.
JULIAN	*(hysterically)* I don't care. It's too much — it's all too much. We haven't been put on this earth to wash his dirty dishes and scrape his porridge saucepans. If we wanted to be unskilled labourers we could be working for Joan Littlewood. I'm not staying in this house another minute. Come on, Sandy — good day, Mr Horne — good day.
F/X	**DOOR SLAMS. DOORBELL RINGS. DOOR OPENS AGAIN.**
Kenneth Horne	Oh it's you again. What is it?
JULIAN	We just wanted to know — what time do you want us tomorrow?
ORCHESTRA	**PAY OFF MUSIC**
	(applause)
Kenneth Horne	And finally, trends in music — what's new in the world of pop?
Kenneth Williams	*(old)* Nothing son, what's new in your world?
Kenneth Horne	Well, climbing the charts are the Fraser Hayes Four who are going to sing a track from their new LP — Alan Breeze at Carnegie Hall. Ladies and gentlemen — The Fraser Hayes Four.
	(applause)
FRASER HAYES FOUR & ORCHESTRA	**MUSIC BREAK**
	(applause)
Kenneth Horne	And now — Episode four of the Clissold Saga.
ORCHESTRA	**FANFARE**
Kenneth Horne	This week we continue the story of Beatrice Clissold — that grand old actress, whom Lionel Hale has called 'The pure brass of the music hall

38

Last week I went, once again, down to her old moss-covered house at Chattering Parva, knocked on her old moss-covered door, which was opened by Spasm, her moss-covered old butler...

F/X	**SPECIAL EFFECTS — FINISHING WITH DOOR CREAKING OPEN**

SPASM
(Kenneth Williams) Be you the white tornado?

Kenneth Horne No, it's just a trick of the light. I'm Kenneth Horne. Could I speak to your mistress?

SPASM No, she be incommunicado —

Kenneth Horne Well, go and shout through the keyhole and tell her I'm here.

SPASM Go back to Lunnon young man! Go home! Get thee hence from this accursed house!
(*building to a scream*) There be nameless horrors here! Ghastly spectres walk abroad at the witching hour. Go home, I tell ee! Go home! Go —
(*slipping into snide voice*) Here, do I have to do all this rubbish week after week?

Kenneth Horne I'm afraid so — it's a sort of running character you see.

SPASM Oh well. (*shouts*) Go home — go home young master. (*chuckles — snide*) Young master!

F/X **HOUND HOWLS**

Kenneth Horne Isn't that the phantom hound? The Hound of the Counterblasts?

SPASM	Aye — that he be. See look! There — he's manifested hisself against the curtains. He often does that. See him! He be a fearsome sight, bain't he? Nearly eight-feet tall he be — with great slavering jaws — and fangs, and eyes like red-hot coals. (*whistles*) Here Spot — Come and and say hello to the nice gen'lman.
F/X	**THUDDING OF HUGE PAWS AND HEAVY PANTING**
Kenneth Horne	Keep him back — don't let him get too near me.
F/X	**HUGE DOG LICKING KENNETH.**
SPASM	I can see he's taken to you. Ah look at him rolling over.
Kenneth Horne	Why is he doing that?
SPASM	He wants you to rub his phantom belly.
Kenneth Horne	What? Like this...?
SPASM	Ar — that's it. He likes that. Look at his phantom leg going like the clappers. Oh he'm a noble beast he is.
Kenneth Horne	Where's he gone? He's disappeared.
SPASM	Ar — he do that often. I think he's gone phantom walkies.
Kenneth Horne	Oh — haunted house trained is he? Look, could I see Lady Counterblast — you see I haven't got all that long.
SPASM	None of us has. We all be doomed. Doomed I tell ee. Doomed. (*drops back into snide voice*) She's in there.
F/X	**DOOR OPENS**
SPASM	Lady Counterblast — tis the young master. (*shouts going off mike*) Doomed, doomed, we be doomed etc.
LADY BEATRICE COUNTERBLAST (Betty Marsden)	I think he's been at the metal polish again.
Kenneth Horne	Well Lady Counterblast, I've been fascinated by the stories you've told me so far — you've known many famous men haven't you?
LADY COUNTERBLAST	Many men. Many many many ... But of all the husbands I've had, the one that sticks in my mind — not to mention my craw — was Sir Arnold Mollusc.
Kenneth Horne	The archaeologist? The man who excavated the tombs of the early Egyptian Kings?
LADY COUNTERBLAST	Yes. I married him in 1922 and we went out to Egypt and together we excavated — many tombs — many many many tombs — many many many ...
Kenneth Horne	But I believe that one such excursion ended in disaster.
LADY COUNTERBLAST	You are referring, of course, to the curse of Tut-En-Asar. Yes, we had pitched camp by an oasis. A small dedicated group. Professor Tippett who led the expedition, my husband and I.
ORCHESTRA	**MUSIC LINK**

40

SIR ARNOLD MOLLUSC (Hugh Paddick)	I can't stand it Beatrice — the heat, the zips.
LADY COUNTERBLAST	(young) Why do you say that dearest?
SIR ARNOLD	We're not allowed to mention flies on the BBC. Professor, can't we turn back?
PROFESSOR TIPPETT (Kenneth Horne)	We must go on. Tomorrow we'll be at the tomb of Tut-En-Asar. Take heart, Mollusc.
SIR ARNOLD	I think I've got a touch of beri-beri.
PROFESSOR TIPPETT	Never mind — when we get back to Europe you can go to Baden-Baden for the cure-cure.
SIR ARNOLD	But the camel drivers won't go on Professor — they say that whoever opens the Mummy's tomb will be struck down by the curse. That's the word all around the camp.
LADY COUNTERBLAST	That's just a lot of camp chat.
SIR ARNOLD	It isn't. They've deserted us. Gone back to Cairo.
PROFESSOR TIPPETT	Sssh. There's someone outside the tent.
SIR ARNOLD	So there is — a strange lumpy figure in a camel hair coat.
LADY COUNTERBLAST	Who is it?
SIR ARNOLD	It's a camel. And there's two Arabs riding it. They're getting off — they're coming towards us. Good heavens, it's a couple of Toerags . . .
LADY COUNTERBLAST	No, darling, you mean Touregs . . .
ABU BEN NEVIS (Kenneth Williams)	Salutations effendi. May your crops not be devoured by locusts and may your herds multiply in abundance. May the moon rise upon your tranquillity and may the sun never set upon your fortune.
SIR ARNOLD	Yes, very kind of you but . . .
ABU BEN NEVIS	For is it not written that as the desert jackal howls at the moon, even so shall the asp lie down with the goat and the camel. And by the beard of Abdul Ben Warriss, may the eagle never defile your caravan, may your concubines bring joy to your heart and may laughter tinkle in your tents and may your loins be fruitful . . .
SIR ARNOLD	Er — yes — and your loins an' all. And with regard to *your* crops and eagles and concubines etc. etc., I hope they find you as it leaves me — er — yours faithfully Arnold Mollusc.
CAMEL DRIVER (Bill Pertwee)	Even so. And may your joys be as numerous as the grains of sand in the . . .
SIR ARNOLD	Look, do we have to go through that again? What are you trying to say?
ABU BEN NEVIS	Would you like to buy some postcards?
SIR ARNOLD	Certainly not.
CAMEL DRIVER	Would you like to meet my sister?
SIR ARNOLD	(mutters) No. I've got the wife with me.

ABU BEN NEVIS	Ah — is this her — she is radiant, a desert flower, a pearl of incomparable price . . .
SIR ARNOLD	No, that's the Professor.
PROFESSOR TIPPETT	Just a trick of the light. Look, what do you want of us?
CAMEL DRIVER	We hear that you're looking for the tomb of Tut-En-Asar. We are guides, perhaps we can help you. Our card . . .
SIR ARNOLD	(reads) 'Desert holidays — Guided Touregs — Single Bedouins in every tent. Constant hot sand. Chauffeur driven camels. Our speciality, tombs defiled.' That's just what we're looking for. So you can lead us to the tomb of Tut-En-Asar? What price are you asking?
CAMEL DRIVER	Well in the desert, money is of no use — we barter. What have you got?
SIR ARNOLD	Well, we've only got a camel.
ABU BEN NEVIS	Oh! That's more than enough. We'll have that. Alright, George — shop!
CAMEL DRIVER	One camel. I'll just ring that up.
F/X	**TINKLE OF CASH REGISTER**
CAMEL DRIVER	Right now, I'm afraid you'll have to have your change in goats.
F/X	**BLEATING OF GOATS**
SIR ARNOLD	No no — keep the change. They'll only weigh my pockets down. Now that's settled — we ride at dawn.
ORCHESTRA	**VERY BRIEF MUSIC LINK**
LADY COUNTERBLAST	(old) And so we set off on camel back — for three days and nights our little caravan filed across the desert. We had only one end in view. That of the camel in front. But then, on the morning of the fourth day, we arrived at our destination — the great pyramid of Tut-En-Asar. (fade — and fade up)
CAMEL DRIVER	Here effendi —
PROFESSOR TIPPETT	Are you sure it's the right tomb?
CAMEL DRIVER	Oh yes, master. See the hieroglyphics on the wall.
PROFESSOR TIPPETT	What do they say Mollusc — you're the expert.
SIR ARNOLD	Let me see now. What's this word. It's spelt duck, duck, crocodile, sacred handmaiden, reaping hook and a dog up to something rather vulgar. Hmmm. That's ancient Egyptian for — High Priest would like to meet falcon-headed god with view to . . . Good gracious! No wonder their civilisation crumbled. I'm going inside.
LADY COUNTERBLAST	What's this inscription underneath — double crocodile, ibis, duck, duck, followed by what looks like Wilson, Keppel and Betty?
SIR ARNOLD	Let me see now — duck — duck — mmm — er, well this is a rough translation but from what I can make out it says — Pharaoh: I say Nefertiti, what's the difference between the back end of a sacred hippopotamus and a letter box? Nefertiti: I don't know. Pharaoh: Well in that case I won't ask you to post my papyrus. We've found it! We've found it!

BBC SOUND ENGINEER, ASSISTANT DEPUTY STAGE MANAGER, OR SOMEONE OF THAT ILK

DOOR TO NEXT PAGE

LADY COUNTERBLAST	What have we found?
SIR ARNOLD	The Riddle of the Sphinx.
PROFESSOR TIPPETT	I don't wish to know that. kindly leave the desert.
SIR ARNOLD	Not before I've opened the tomb.
ABU BEN NEVIS	Do not open the tomb effendi. For is it not written that he who desecrates the tomb of Tut-En-Asar shall be stricken with the Mummy's curse and shall be consumed by the seven plagues, fire, scorpions, locusts, serpents, vermin and cramp in the knees? Is it not so written by the High Priest of Ibis?
SIR ARNOLD	Is it?
ABU BEN NEVIS	Course not. I just made it up.
PROFESSOR TIPPETT	Nevertheless, there is a curse on the tomb.
SIR ARNOLD	I don't care — we've come all this way — I'm not turning back now. I'm going in. Give me a hand with this door.
F/X	**CREAKING OF STONE DOOR OPENING FOLLOWED BY HOLLOW FOOTSTEPS**
SIR ARNOLD	Good heavens. It's incredible in here. You'll never guess what I've found — I've just found an . . . (*startled*) eeeeeeek!
ORCHESTRA	**MUSIC LINK**
LADY COUNTERBLAST	(*old*) By the time I got to him, poor Arnold, he was quite dead.
Kenneth Horne	The curse of the Mummy had struck.

LADY COUNTERBLAST	We found him lying there with an asp clasped in his grasp.
ORCHESTRA	**PAY OFF**
	(*applause*)
Kenneth Horne	What a thrill packed load of old twaddle. Well, that's all for this week, except to announce the winner of our limerick competition. Last week, you may recall, we supplied the first two lines and asked you to complete the limerick. This is the winning entry: An animal breeder called Gluck Once crossbred a hamster and duck. When asked for a name For this beast of ill-fame He said, it's a web-footed huck.
	And so to Mrs Runcible of Cheshire goes this week's prize. A box of novelties and games including the Vanishing Lady Trick, The Magic Handkerchief Trick and the amazing disappearing Christmas pudding with instructions on how to work it.
	Cheerio — see you next week.
	(*applause*)
ORCHESTRA	**'ROUND THE HORNE' PLAY OUT**

ROUND THE HORNE

2ND SERIES — PROGRAMME NO. 1
TRANSMISSION: Sunday 13th March 1966:
1.30-2.00 p.m. LIGHT PROGRAMME

Hugh Paddick	(*cockney*) I see Round the Horne's on in a minute, Dad.
Kenneth Williams	(*very very old*) Muck that is Muck. I wouldn't pollute me ears with it.
Hugh Paddick	I think it's quite clever, the way they do them voices — that Kenneth Williams —
Kenneth Williams	Muck he is. Downright muck. They're all muck, every one of them.
Hugh Paddick	That Kenneth Horne isn't. He's educated.
Kenneth Williams	Well he ought to know better, consorting with that other muck. It's all double entendres, incinuendoes and catchpenny horseplay.
Hugh Paddick	So you're not going to have it on?
Kenneth Williams	No. I shall just sit here and polish me boots with the cat.

Hugh Paddick	Alright dad, but I think you should listen.
Kenneth Williams	Why? Give me one good reason?
Hugh Paddick	Well, you are the Head of Broadcasting.
Kenneth Williams	Alright — switch it on — but it's a load of muck.
ORCHESTRA	**SIGNATURE TUNE**
	(*applause*)
Hugh Paddick	Ladies and Gentlemen — the programme that contains ninety-nine percent of all known jokes — Round The Horne.
ORCHESTRA	**SIGNATURE TUNE UP**

Douglas Smith	The story so far — the Japs were getting nearer. Brutal drill-pig sergeant Hugh Paddick — a regular now for the last twenty-one years (thanks to Boggis's Fruit Salts) crouched in a fox hole. Nearby, a fox, played by nimble Betty Marsden in a skin, crouched in a Hugh Paddick hole which she'd just dug. The Sergeant looked at his two companions — second lieutenant Bill Pertwee, he of the apple cheeks and pear-shaped body, and boyish, wistful Kenneth Williams, bent as always under the weight of the Vickers machine gun he'd borrowed from the Vicar. 'Would relief never come' thought Paddick. Suddenly Williams leapt to his feet, and unbuckling the Sam Browne belt that held up Sam Browne's trousers and brandishing them above his head, he cried, 'I'm going over the top'. The censor got him before he'd gone two yards. The two survivors crouched there — then suddenly when all seemed lost, they heard the cry that told them that the long awaited succour was on its way —
Kenneth Horne	Good evening. This is the long awaited sucker — Kenneth Horne.
ORCHESTRA	**MUSIC**
	(*applause over*)
Kenneth Horne	That was Douglas Smith, England's only nudist Kosher butcher and man-about-town. The town, of course being West Hartlepools. Well now, as this is the first of a brand new series, here are the answers to last week's questions. The answer to question one — complete the first lines of the following songs — 'If I were a blackbird I'd . . . .' The answer is 'I'd whistle and sing', and I positively will not accept any other suggestions. The second song was 'There's a rainbow round my . . . .' Now we got an amazing number of replies to this. We haven't had so many since we asked you to complete 'Over My Shoulder Goes . . . .' Really it makes it very difficult for us to keep up the high reputation for sophisticated comedy that we've never had. And now back again hot foot from his thick army socks comes that debonair yobbo, Douglas Smith.
Douglas Smith	Hello again fans. And now the further adventures of Kenneth Horne — Master Spy.
ORCHESTRA	**MUSIC**
Kenneth Horne	I sat at the gaming table of my club — The White Orang Utan in Jermyn Street. I'd been losing heavily at chemmy — and not for the first time the thought crossed my mind — 'I wish I could chemmy like my sister Kate'. I was in trouble and I knew it. Opposite me sat my adversary — The Head of Stench, whose initials stood for 'Special Executive for Terrorism, Extortion, Nuclear Counter Espionage and Hand Laundry'. So this was Kronkmeyer, the arch criminal. He spoke —
KRONKMEYER (Kenneth Williams)	Come on Mr Horne, ducky, your deal —
Kenneth Horne	I beg your pardon? Where does 'ducky' come in?
Kenneth Williams	I interpolated it. After all you *said* arch. If you wanted a butch criminal you only had to say so. I can be as butch as the next man, can't I?
Hugh Paddick	(*fey*) Course you can.
Kenneth Williams	See? I'm not limited, am I. I've got range — I'm versatile.
Hugh Paddick	Bottomless, his versatility is. He can run the gamut. Run your gamut for him. Do your act. The one you do in the clubs up North.

Kenneth Williams	(*as north country impersonator*) Alright. Ladies and Gentlemen of Greaseborough — I went to a Hollywood party the other night with my roving microphone. Well here I am at a Hollywood party and who's that over there? Why it's Tom Mix talking to lovely Theda Bara. (*American voice*) Hello lovely Theda Bara. (*deep gruff voice*) Hello Tom Mix.
Kenneth Horne	Did Theda Bara really sound like that?
Kenneth Williams	Yes. That's what ruined her when talkies came in. Don't interrupt. Pushing my way through the throngs of celebrities — Excuse me Fatty Arbuckle, pardon me D.W. Griffiths — why who is that I see now deep in conversation in the corner — why it's the late great George Arliss talking to the late great Al Jolson. (*Arliss*) Hello late great Al Jolson. Why don't you sing us a song in your inimitable way. (*Jolson*) Alright late great George Arliss. (*sings*) Mammy, Mammy, I'd walk a million miles if I had your —

Kenneth Horne	Excuse me — I don't want to appear stuffy but we're in the middle of a James Bond parody. I don't quite see a place for the late great Al Jolson — unless we play the sketch as a seance. I mean, you've only got one line — no need to make a meal of it.
URIAH HEAP (Bill Pertwee)	I'll do it Mr Horne. I'm very humble. I'm grateful for anything. Please Mr Horne, please — however menial it is, I'll do it — I'm humble you see, humble.
Hugh Paddick	Oh here we go — the welcome return of Uriah Pertwee.
URIAH HEAP	(*slipping into yokel or vice versa*) Did you hear that, Mr Horne. The way they sneer at me cos I'm a provincial. That Hugh Paddick with his glib London ways — and that Mr Williams. He's a Piccadilly Johnny he is. They look down on me — they laugh at my rude moleskin trousers and my clumsy manners. They mock me cos I'm not one of the fancy, but who would fancy anyone in rude moleskin trousers —
Kenneth Williams	A rude mole.
URIAH HEAP	(*dropping further into appalling rural accent*) Yes — you hates me Master Kenneth, you always did. Cos Miss Sibling up

	the hall preferred me to you. Ay, she spurned thee for oi — Ar — Aha — ar ahar. (*Suddenly switching to breezy compere voice*) And now ladies and gentlemen — The Hunchback of Notre Dame — (*guttural voice*) Why am I so ugly — why am I so ugly?
Betty Marsden	Answers please on a postcard to Round The Horne — Care of the BBC, Ghana.
Kenneth Horne	Please, Betty, don't you start. I thought I could rely on you.
Betty Marsden	(*as Duchess of Malfi*) Yes, you thought you'd bought my loyalty — with a plate of oysters and a bottle of milk stout. (*starts to shout*) I was a good girl till I met him. Selling flowers in Covent Garden I was. Then 'e come along. 'E had a wager with his fine gen'lman friend, Colonel Edwin Braden —
Kenneth Williams	Great hairy fool!
Betty Marsden	He said I'd never be a lydy while I kept dropping me aspirates — he said he'd pass me off as a duchess.
Hugh Paddick	He promised me the same thing —
Kenneth Williams	Any luck?
Hugh Paddick	Well — so-so, but between ourselves I think the Duke's beginning to suspect something.
ORCHESTRA	**CYMBAL CRASH — INTO VARIETY TYPE PAYOFF MUSIC IN FAST TWO**
Betty Marsden	Mike and Bernie Winters are now appearing in 'Bareskins and Frolics' at the Opera House, Glyndebourne.
Douglas Smith	Meanwhile, back at the plot —
Kenneth Horne	Kronkmeyer and I stared across the gaming table at each other. His eyes smouldered fiercely. I stubbed them out in an ashtray. My losses were heavy. I pulled out my bankbook — my adversary smiled —
KRONKMEYER (Kenneth Williams)	You are acquainted with the game of chess I believe, Mr Horne —
Kenneth Horne	Yes.
KRONKMEYER	Then of course you understand the term 'checkmate'.
Kenneth Horne	Then you meant . . .
KRONKMEYER	Yes. You know what you can do with your cheque mate.
Kenneth Horne	Kronkmeyer's hand snaked under his jacket and re-emerged holding something small, black and shiny that I recognised with a tremor of fear.
KRONKMEYER	You know what this is, Mr Horne?
Kenneth Horne	Yes, a pickled walnut.
KRONKMEYER	Precisely. And I'm not afraid to use it.
Kenneth Horne	There was only one thing could save me now. I had to go for my gun. Excuse me Kronkmeyer, I have to go for my gun.

KRONKMEYER	Well hurry back. I can't hang about here all night clutching a soggy pickled walnut.
Kenneth Horne	I slipped out into the bar. It had been a close call. I knew that the next time we met, Kronkmeyer and I would have to have a reckoning. I propped my long lean form against the bar, and sat on a stool next to it. The swarthy barman smiled and showed me his gold teeth —
Hugh Paddick	(*gummy*) Here you are — have a look at my gold teeth.
Kenneth Horne	Very nice. Now just slip them back and get me a drink — I'll have my usual — a small glass of Parrish's Chemical Food — stirred but not shaken. I drank it in one gulp — I was shaken but not stirred. At that moment a waiter sidled over, sneezed discreetly into my drink and whispered up my nose. It was the message I had been expecting. 'M' wanted to see me — at once. I hailed a passing announcer and told him to step on it. Smith?
Douglas Smith	Yes sir?
Kenneth Horne	Step on it will you.
Douglas Smith	Very good sir.
F/X	**SOMETHING NASTY BEING CRUNCHED UNDERFOOT**
Douglas Smith	There — I've stepped on it — it's quite dead now.
Kenneth Horne	Good — then announce me to the Headquarters of M.I.5.
Douglas Smith	Certainly sir. Five minutes later — outside a small back room in the top security wing of Whitehall.
F/X	**KNOCK ON DOOR**
Betty Marsden	(*Russian off mike*) Come in Comrade.
F/X	**DOOR OPENS**
Kenneth Horne	'M's' new secretary sat behind the desk. I surveyed her briefly and recommended immediate possession. She had everything a tough virile man could want — big biceps, a huge black beard — not formally good looking but interesting to a certain kind of man — Bertram Mills, Billy Smart, Barnum and Bailey. She spoke again —
Betty Marsden	(*Russian*) If you wish to see the decadent Imperialist Capitalist hyena, I'll tell him you're here.
Kenneth Horne	She waved me in the direction of the office with her Communist Party membership card — there was something wrong — what was she doing here? I would have to ask 'M'. I strode into his office. He was bent over his work, but off duty, straight as a die.
'M' (Hugh Paddick)	Ah Horne — glad you've come. I've just had these plates sent over from the lab. What do you make of them?
Kenneth Horne	Mmm. Baked beans I'd say.
'M'	Just as I thought. The food in the canteen gets worse and worse every day.
Kenneth Horne	That girl outside, your new secretary —
'M'	You mean Gladys?

Kenneth Horne	Yes. Has she defected recently?
'M'	Well none of us is perfect. No. She's a double agent for SMERSH and WHOOSH.
Kenneth Horne	WHOOSH?
'M'	A new detergent. But we've got something more important to worry about. Here — take these binoculars — look out of this window at the Houses of Parliament — what do you see?
Kenneth Horne	I see the Earl of Arran's at it again —
'M'	No. Look at Big Ben.
Kenneth Horne	That's not Big Ben. What is it?
'M'	It's just coming up to twelve o'clock — Listen.
F/X	**LOUD WHIRRING OF CLOCK MACHINERY — INCLUDING VERY LOUD TICKING AND THEN — HUGE DEEP 'CUCKOO — CUCKOO'.**

Kenneth Horne	Good heavens — a fifty-foot high cuckoo.
'M'	Yes. Someone's stolen Big Ben and substituted a mechanical cuckoo — at least we hope it's mechanical. You realise what this means to the Empire — No Big Ben!
Kenneth Horne	Yes. The end of the Big Ben Banjo Band as we know it.
'M'	Precisely. So far we've managed to cover it up. The BBC have been very cooperative. Before the nine o'clock news, Sir Hugh Greene himself comes into the studio and shouts 'Bong Bong' but if the poor chap gets laryngitis, it'll be civil war.
Kenneth Horne	Who would have taken Big Ben? I mean it'd be very difficult to get it out of the country.
'M'	Yes — we've alerted the police and customs officials to be on the look out for a very tall man with an enormous bulge in his waistcoat pocket. We have one slight clue to the identity of the thief — a visiting card left at the scene of the crime. Here —
Kenneth Horne	(*reading*) 'Doctor Chou En Ginsberg, International Clock Thief — 14 Station Parade, Switzerland.' Hm — not much to go on. But why Switzerland?
'M'	I think the scriptwriters are planning some dreadful joke about the Matterhorn. Be on your guard against it. Now you'll need some special equipment — Colonel Haverstrap of stores will be glad to fill you in — he's never liked you.
Kenneth Horne	The interview was over. 'M' smiled at me wryly — I smiled at his O'Hara — then together the two Irishmen, Riley and O'Hara swaggered off arm in arm in the direction of Kilburn. I hurried to the bottom of the page where Colonel Haverstrap was waiting for me, disguised as a greasy thumbprint.
COLONEL HAVERSTRAP (Bill Pertwee)	(*gruff army N.C.O. type*) Alright Horne — here's your equipment. These are your small arms, these are your puny hairy legs and this is your tiny bald head — you know how to use them I take it. Here's a plastic Japanese junior spy kit, comprising a small plastic dagger, the egg in bag trick, a revolving bow tie, nail through finger trick, an exploding banjo — and this...
Kenneth Horne	Good heavens — what is it?
COLONEL HAVERSTRAP	Ah well, the trade name is — Naughty Doggie — Fido Gets The Blame. Only use it if you're in a tight corner.
Kenneth Horne	How does it help me escape?
COLONEL HAVERSTRAP	While they're beating the daylights out of the dog, you can slip out unnoticed. But if there's no other way out — use this card — but remember, you can only use it once.
Kenneth Horne	(*reads*) Get out of jail free.
COLONEL HAVERSTRAP	That's all then Horne, except for these — a gun that looks like a transistor radio — a transistor radio that looks like a gun — and...
ORCHESTRA	**DRAMATIC MUSIC**
COLONEL HAVERSTRAP	.......this umbrella.

Kenneth Horne	Mmm. A cunning device. What's it for?
LONEL HAVERSTRAP	To keep the rain off, you bald-headed fool! Right. Good luck Horne. There's a plane leaving London Airport for Switzerland in eight bars time — Be on it.
ORCHESTRA	FAST MUSIC LINK
Kenneth Horne	I relaxed in the luxury first class compartment of the Super Constellation Pan World Airways Swept Wing Sopwith Camel that was to take me to my rendezvous with fate. The hostess bent over me.
AIR HOSTESS (Betty Marsden)	We're about to take off sir. Would you like a boiled sweet or cotton wool?
Kenneth Horne	I won't have the boiled sweets. They just fall out of my ears. I'll just have some cotton wool.
AIR HOSTESS	Here you are, sir.
Kenneth Horne	Thank you. (*sound of munching*) Delicious. Then suddenly I realised, too late, the cotton wool had been impregnated with a sleep inducing drug manufactured from a blend of poppy seed, liquorice and senna pods. Well to be honest, it didn't induce sleep, but it seemed the safest thing to do. My head spun and then blackness engulfed me.
GRAMS	SHORT DRAMATIC SWEEP OF STRINGS
Kenneth Horne	When I came to, I found myself in a bare room strapped to an operating table. A face swam into focus — an evil yellow face that I knew to be that of my adversary — the inscrutable Doctor Chou En Ginsberg.
CHOU EN GINSBURG (Kenneth Williams)	Ah Mr Horne — so we meet again — etcetera blah blah blah —
Kenneth Horne	Why do you say that Ginsberg?
CHOU EN GINSBURG	While you were unconscious we cut twelve pages. You are being kept plisoner in underglound seclet labolatoly. Yes, Mr Horne — I lead the question in your eyes —
Kenneth Horne	Thank heavens, I thought, he hasn't spotted the one up my nose.
CHOU EN GINSBERG	Yes, Mr Horne — I stole Blig Blen.
Kenneth Horne	But why? Why?
CHOU EN GINSBERG	(*screams*) Because I wanted to undermine foundations of Blitish Empire — because I wanted to show I am most powerful man in whole universe! (*snide*) Besides, my Mickey Mouse wrist watch has broken. But you will never live to tell Horne — you are going to die — but before you die you will be tortured. Aha — aha — oho — aha. (*snide*) There's about another half dozen of those but I think we can take it as read. Alright, Mr Horne, I clap hands (*claps hands*) and here comes Charlie.
LOTUS BLOSSOM (Hugh Paddick)	Yers guv?
Kenneth Horne	Good heavens — isn't that your concubine, Lotus Blossom?
CHOU EN GINSBERG	Yes. But changed name by deed poll. Neighbours starting to talk. Now known as Charlie Girl, from hit musical of same name . . . 'I laughed till

	my sides ached' Halold Hobson, Sunday Times. Now my little bamboo . . . shoot — my little Tsai double Tchin . . .
LOTUS BLOSSOM	Yers oh mighty mandarin — what is your bidding — I await your behest.
CHOU EN GINSBERG	I'm never at my behest at this time of morning. Go my little nightingale and prepare the torture.
LOTUS BLOSSOM	Yes oh warlord. I run like a fleet gazelle.
F/X	**HEAVY CLUMPING OF BOOTS RUNNING INTO DISTANCE**
CHOU EN GINSBERG	If you can imagine a fleet gazelle with hobnailed boots on. Now Mr Horne, I shall leave you to await my little friend on whom no man has looked and lived. Goodbye Mr Horne — we'll meet again, don't know where, don't know when (*sings in nasal Vera Lynn tones*) — but I know we'll meet again some sunny day.
F/X	**DOOR CLOSES**
Kenneth Horne	I was alone. I thought 'Horne — this is it'. I started to saw through my bonds — somewhere in Pinewood, Bond started to saw through his Hornes. When you're in Show Business you help each other. Then the door creaked open — a strange wild haired creature with insane staring eyes and great . . . fangs stood there. It opened its huge revenous maw and from its throat issued a spine chilling sound which made my blood turn cold . . .
Bill Pertwee	(*as Ken Dodd, sings*) Tears have been my only consolation . . .
ORCHESTRA	**MUSIC UP TO CLIMAX**
	(*applause over music*)
ORCHESTRA	**'KENNETH HORNE MASTER SPY' THEME — UNDER FOLLOWING ANNOUNCEMENT . . .**
Douglas Smith	(*over music*) That was Episode One of Kenneth Horne — Master Spy. Will his reason snap under the strain of Ken Dodd's singing — or will he escape and continue his pursuit of Big Ben? Will Chou En Ginsberg triumph over Justice? Will Arkle win the Cheltenham Gold Cup and Will ye no come back again. Tune in next week when we bring you Episode Two of Kenneth Horne — Master Spy.
ORCHESTRA	**MUSIC UP AND OUT**
Kenneth Horne	And here to pile their peculiar brand of pelion on this load of old ossa — it's alright, it's not dirty, I looked it up — are the Fraser Hayes Four to sing you a track from their new L.P. 'The Tijuana Brass at the Bow Street Magistrates Court' — Ladies and Gentlemen — The Fraser Hayes Four.
FRASER HAYES FOUR & ORCHESTRA	**MUSIC BREAK**
	(*applause*)
Kenneth Horne	Thank you the Plastic Fraser Hayes Four.
Douglas Smith	And now the part of the show that keeps you up to date with what today's people are doing — Trends!

ORCHESTRA	TRENDS MUSIC
Kenneth Horne	First — the World of Art.
DAPHNE WHITETHIGH (Betty Marsden)	Pop's out —
Kenneth Horne	Well pop it back in again and let's get on with the show. Next, fashio
DAPHNE WHITETHIGH	Balenciaga's dropped his skirts again.
Kenneth Horne	Bad luck Balenciaga! And what are the trendy people doing?
Hugh Paddick	(*Guards Officer voice*) Jean Shrimpton still has that indescribable Stam about her.
DAPHNE WHITETHIGH	Actress Samantha Eggar is rumoured to be starting a company to promo her career — It is to be called the Eggar Marketing Board.
Hugh Paddick	(*Guards Officer voice*) So why not go to work on an Eggar?
Kenneth Horne	Still leading the pop music trend is that doyen of folk singers, Ramblin Syd Rumpo. We asked him to come along and sing some of his songs tonight but, unfortunately, he could — and here he is — Rambling Sy Rumpo.
RAMBLING SYD (Kenneth Williams)	Well now my deario — oh sing willow tit willow for I've crumpled m doddle-oh.
Kenneth Horne	Oh really, how painful for you. I'll give you the address of my garage.
RAMBLING SYD	I was just being picturesque as is my wont. For I wander along life's highways a'culling of the simple folk melodies of our island heritage a a'cleaning 'em up for Saturday Club oh — A'posset me bodkin till I rumble me groats and the old grey goose is gone — oh, although to b frank I was glad to see the back of her.
Kenneth Horne	And what are you going to sing us this week?
RAMBLING SYD	Tis a hoary old folk song that I picked up from a home for hoary old folks. Tis a courting song or air which tells of the coming of Spring t Clapham Junction and tis about this young swain of they parts who ever Spring feels the sap rising and gets a kind of March Madness which is common to the young men of they parts and is known as swain fever. H wanders among the bosky haunts and verdant pasture-lands of Clapha High Street and as he hears the little hedge sparrow coughing and sees th young lambs hanging up in the butchers shop, he feels a primaeval urg And he goes forth to seek his true love. Suddenly he spies this winsom creature sitting in a window, with flaxen tresses flowing in the breeze. A he stands under the window in the moonlight, plighting his troth — an he sings — 'If you will marry me my love, I will give you a ruby ring, single rose, a peacock in a cage, the moon to wear for a garland in you hair and three books of green stamps'. And then the object of his desir looks all haughty at him, and tossing back the flaxen ringlets, sings th plaintive lament:

GUITAR ACCOMPANIMENT

Tho' you give me a single rose
And a ruby ring to wear — oh
A peacock in a cage of gold
And moonbeams for my hair — oh

I cannot marry thee sir,
I cannot marry thee sir,
For I am promised to someone else —
Besides, I am a geezer.
Geezer.
Geezer —
Because I am a geee-eee-zer —
oooooOOOh! I think I've ricked meself!

(applause)

Kenneth Horne	Thank you Rambling Syd — And they say romance is dead. Now for trendy people, the final accolade is to appear on one of the late night television shows where exciting, fun, with-it, super type people get together and make boring, flat conversation for an hour. I tuned in last Sunday night, just in time to hear . . .
ORCHESTRA	**CHAT SHOW TYPE MUSIC 'SEAMUS ANDROID'**
Douglas Smith	And now — embalmed from London — The Seamus Android Show —
GRAMS	**APPLAUSE**
ORCHESTRA	**FADE SIGNATURE TUNE**
Hugh Paddick	*(cheery announcer)* And tonight Seamus's guests are Anatole de Gruntfuttock, the celebrated dog forger, Puberty Griswold 'the Boxing Rabbi', pop-singer Ruff Trayde and the Cruisers, and philosopher and racing tipster Captain Spock of the Nudist Racing Pink — and here is your host — Seamus Android —
GRAMS	**APPLAUSE**
SEAMUS ANDROID (Bill Pertwee)	Well now, we've got a really dull show for you tonight, and you'll be meeting some extremely lifeless nonentities with some off-the-cuff Sunday night rubbish that I'm sure will bore the pants off ya. My first guest is one of the original Gaiety Girls and now starring in a new West End musical at the age of ninety-eight — Gladys Runt!
ORCHESTRA	**MUSIC**
GRAMS	**APPLAUSE**
SEAMUS ANDROID	Well Gladys, you're ninety-eight — how does it feel . . . .
GLADYS RUNT (Betty Marsden)	I can't remember —
SEAMUS ANDROID	. . . . to be back in the West End? You must have some wonderful memories.
GLADYS RUNT	Yes, I have. I have some very wonderful memories. Some very very wonderful memories.
SEAMUS ANDROID	Really? Is that so. Well, would you like to tell us some of your wonderful memories.
GLADYS RUNT	I'd like to. I'd like to very much. But I can't remember them.
SEAMUS ANDROID	But surely there is an anecdote told about you and Bernard Shaw?
GLADYS RUNT	Oh yes — that one. Well, I was playing in Captain Brassbound's Conversation — and one night Mr Shaw himself watched the performance

from the wings — when I came off we stood together for a few momer
and then he leant very close to me and whispered in my ear — in that
gracious way of his — he said — 'Get off my foot you silly old tart'.

SEAMUS ANDROID   Well, that's all we've got time for this week. But tune in again next wee
when you'll be meeting some more Sunday night people who make yo
long for Monday morning.

ORCHESTRA   **CHAT SHOW TYPE PLAY OFF**

(applause)

Kenneth Horne	There's nothing like good conversation and I think you'll agree that the Seamus Android Show is just that. Nothing like good conversation. The trouble with trends is that they change so often. And so last week I thought it was time to pay another visit to Carnaby Street to equip myself with a new wardrobe — so, taking my Courrège in both hands I went along to a men's boutique that calls itself 'Bona Drag'.
F/X	SHOP BELL
Kenneth Horne	Hello — Anybody there?
JULIAN (Hugh Paddick)	Hello — I'm Julian and this is my friend, Sandy.
SANDY (Kenneth Williams)	Oh it's Mr Horne — how fabe — I thought you'd retired.
Kenneth Horne	Retired? Didn't you see me on television last week?
SANDY	Yes, that's what made me think. Well how bona to vada your eek again. Of course we're only filling in here between acting jobs. But it's been a bit slack lately.
JULIAN	Sand had a tickle from the tenants last week.
Kenneth Horne	What H.M. Tennant the Impressario?
JULIAN	No, the tenants upstairs. The ones on his half-landing. They're in advertising. They got us a commercial on telly — you may have seen it — we just do the voices.
SANDY	Jule says, in this great gruff voice, it doesn't come natural to him, does it Jule?
JULIAN	No, I'm more your light baritone.
SANDY	He says 'What you doing?' And then I say 'I'm the pea that can't get into the packet'.
JULIAN	Into the packet. Took his part lovely. He makes a very convincing pea. Anyway, Mr Horne, what can we do for you?
Kenneth Horne	Well, with all these new clothes coming out, I thought it was about time I got up to scratch.
JULIAN	Don't let us stop you. Yes, well I think Sand and I can show you something fairly kinky if you hang on for a second —
Kenneth Horne	Thank you. And I'd like to see some clothes as well.
SANDY	Oh bold! Now let's see — to start with — what would be really unusual in a gents suit?
Kenneth Horne	Danny la Rue?
SANDY	I think we'll treat that crude pleasantry with the contempt it deserves, don't you Jule? How about a nice casual jacket?
JULIAN	Yes, D.B., knitted, reefer or lumber?
SANDY	Oh lumber. He's definitely a lumber type. A right lumber. Here's a nice paisley army-style battledress jacket.

Kenneth Horne	Army style?
JULIAN	Yes. We call it Aldershot Camp. Would you like to try it on?
Kenneth Horne	Right. There — what do you think?
SANDY	Well, I don't know — it's quite cheeky isn't it?
JULIAN	Cheeky yes — quite cheeky — it cocks a snook at convention round collar and cuffs.
SANDY	Collar and cuffs, yes. And it provides him with that modern anti-hero peacock look with its hunky arrogance —
JULIAN	Hunky arrogance — yes. It proclaims his empathy with the nouvelle vague.

SANDY	Nouvelle-vague, yes.
Kenneth Horne	Yes, I must admit that it's sybaritically autocratic but it tends to bind under the armpits. Haven't you got anything more conservative?
SANDY	Only in bespoke. Go on Jule, show him your swatch.
JULIAN	What again — Well, there's your denim, comes nice in your burnt marmalade.
SANDY	All the browns are very fetching. Comes beautiful in your donkey. And then there's your silks; you have the shot silk, the wild silk — well fair wild — and then there's the raw. How do you think he'd look in the raw Jule?

JULIAN	I'm not besotted by the idea. The fawn tweed's nice. Why not fawn?
SANDY	On him? I wouldn't cheapen meself. I've got it — show him your Op.
Kenneth Horne	No thank you, I've just had breakfast.
JULIAN	Op Art. Here we are — PVC with bull's-eyes all over it. Very trendy and inner than in, isn't it Sand?
SANDY	Fantabulosa! We can do that for you ready-made. Here — try this on — it's a PVC raincoat.
JULIAN	And you'll want these PVC thigh length boots.
SANDY	Oh and here — a PVC cap to complete your toute plastic ensemble. There — look at yourself in the mirror. What do you think?
Kenneth Horne	I look like an eccentric fireman, but I suppose if it's the thing to wear, I'd better have it — one problem though, how do I get it dry cleaned?
SANDY	You don't. But don't worry — we have an arrangement with the garage next door. As soon as it gets grubby, you just nip into the five minute car wash and half-a-dozen Pakistanis'll hose you down.
ORCHESTRA	PUNCTUATION CHORD

(*applause*)

| Kenneth Horne | So that's what I did. I popped into the Car Wash — and while I was at it I had some anti-freeze put in. Well that's the end of this week's show, except for a police message. If any passer-by in Lisle Street last Saturday night witnessed a middle-aged man stagger out of the Peeperama strip club and get knocked down by a passing cyclist, would you please keep quiet about it as my wife thinks I was in Folkestone. Goodbye. See you next week. |

(*applause*)

| ORCHESTRA | 'ROUND THE HORNE' PLAY OUT |

ROUND THE HORNE

2ND SERIES—PROGRAMME NO. 8
TRANSMISSION: Sunday 1st May 1966:
1.30-2.00 p.m. LIGHT PROGRAMME

Douglas Smith   Here is an important message for all horses — the makers of Dobbiro magic horse rejuvenators announce some new exciting additions to the range —

Hugh Paddick   Is your horse overweight? He can look five pounds lighter in a Dobbi horse-cummerbund.

ANOTHER SATISFE
DOBBITEX
WEARER!

Bill Pertwee	(*child*) What keeps your hooves so soft, Mummy?
Betty Marsden	I always wash in Dobbins Fairy Horse Powder.
Kenneth Williams	When my horse meets his friends for a drink at the Hilton, what does he say?
Bill Pertwee	Dobbi Pratt.
Douglas Smith	And now the show that nine out of ten horses prefer — Round The Horne.
ORCHESTRA	**SIGNATURE TUNE**
Douglas Smith	The story so far: Still on the trail of the Whistling Mouse Nobbler, nightclub hostess Otto Von Potroast, disguised as a Trappist ferret breeder, makes his way on skis to the top of the Eiffel Tower where he believes that Oblivia Nightsong is being held prisoner in a disused plate of curried rice by evil Captain Eric Spong, late of the 14th Light Mounted Viennese Sewers. But who is Cloggpotter? Where are Dimitri's trousers? Why did the man with the metal nose behave so strangely with McWhirter's blancmange? Here is the man who, alone, will answer none of these questions and several others besides — Kenneth Horne.
ORCHESTRA	**MUSIC**
	(*applause*)
Kenneth Horne	That was Douglas Smith, who wishes it to be known . . . But from the way he's been acting lately, it's pretty obvious.
	Now for the answers to last week's questions. First, the odd man out. The answer was, of course, Kenneth Wolstenholme — all the others can be stretched to twice their length.
	Next was the 'complete the lines from the following songs'. First, 'I'm going to wash . . .' Well, the answer was 'that man right out of my hair' and not 'a lady in Barnstaple's washing for three weeks' — but thank you and a nice try Mr Alan Freeman.
	The second song was 'I'm singing in the . . .' Well E.K. of the Dwellings, Rotherhithe, your suggestion, while inaccurate, was interesting. I suppose you have to sing in there if the lock's broken. The correct word, however, was 'rain'. Finally we had 'I get a kick out of . . .' Well, Mr Gruntfuttock of Hoxton, I think we *all* know what you get a kick out of. And on looking at the list you sent me, it's my considered opinion that you are running a severe risk of doing yourself a permanent injury. Besides it doesn't scan. You can't sing —
	(*sings*)
	So tell me how can it be true That I get a kick out of drinking metal polish strained through a football sock.
	Alright, Smith, make the announcement.
Douglas Smith	This is strangely attractive, leggy, gamin Douglas Smith announcing a new feature — The Kenneth Horne Theatre of Suspense.
GRAMS	**ELECTRONIC TYPE MUSIC**
Hugh Paddick	(*sinister*) Somewhere between waking and sleeping, between the conscious and the unconscious, between Hounslow and Hammersmith Broadway lies an area of the mind where strange things happen. Come with us now

65

through the gateway of the supernatural, up the eerie passage of fanta
and through the creaking door of —

F/X   **DOOR KNOB BEING RATTLED**

Hugh Paddick   (*own voice*) Hello, there's someone in the libido. (*shouts*) How long a
you going to stay in there, mate? Other people want to use it.

F/X   **CREAKING DOOR**

Hugh Paddick   Through the creaking door of the libido into the area we call (*sinister
cackle*) — The Twilight Sanctum —

GRAMS   **ELECTRONIC MUSIC UP AND OUT**

SIR GLADYS HARBINGER   My name is Gladys Harbinger. Sir Gladys Harbinger. How I came by tha
(Kenneth Horne)   name is of no importance to the present narrative, so mind your own
business. I am the last of the Harbingers, at least that's what my father sa
when I was born. My mother hails from a small village in Cornwall an
it's said that on a clear day you can hear her for miles.
I was on a brass-rubbing holiday in the West Country, when the events
am about to relate took place. It was a cold October night; my car had
broken down and I was miles from Looe. I decided to make the best of th
situation and look for lodgings in the neighbourhood. A distant light
guided me over the lonely downs to an old Inn, set back off the road.

F/X   **HOWLING WIND.**
CRUNCH OF FOOTSTEPS ON GRAVEL.
DOORBELL CHIMES. RATTLE OF CHAINS AND BOLTS.
HUGE DOOR CREAKS OPEN.

SPASM   Who be you? Be you the egg-chick that be coming my way?
(Kenneth Williams)

SIR GLADYS   Well, not exactly.

SPASM   Be ye man or be ye ghastly manifestation — because if ye be man, ye
welcome here, but if ye be ghastly manifestation, use the tradesman's
entrance. I don't want ectoplasm all over my clean lino.

SIR GLADYS   Actually I was looking for a bed for the night.

SPASM   Get thee gone from this doomed place. We all be doomed here. We've a
got a touch of the doom. There be things here that'd make the hair on yo
legs turn white with fear. I've seen things. I've heard things. I've touche
things. I've smelled things. Don't 'ee ask me what I've seen or heard o
touched or smelled because I wouldn't tell 'ee. Wild horses wouldn't dr
it out of me. No, don't ask, don't ask!

SIR GLADYS   I wasn't going to.

SPASM   Don't 'ee ask me about the Headless Horseman — how 'ee comes
a-gallopin' by about this time. See, there he be now.

SIR GLADYS   Where?

SPASM   He's just manifested hisself in the rhododendron bushes . . .

F/X   **GALLOPING HOOVES START**

SPASM   There — there he goes — a-gallopin' towards the five-bar gate.

F/X	**SPLINTERING OF WOOD**
SPASM	He be fine on the flat, but he'm be useless over the sticks. See the trouble be the horse be headless an' all. They just aren't equipped for the job. But I'm forgetting my manners — come in young master — old Jem's not used to company. Old Jem'll make ye right welcome; nothing's too much trouble for Old Jem.
SIR GLADYS	I'm glad to hear it.
SPASM	Unfortunately it be Old Jem's night off, so you'll have to put up with me. I be Mad Tom Thighblast. If you be set on staying the night in this accursed place, I'll get my wife to show 'ee to your chamber. (*shouts*) Quivering Meg? There be a stranger here.
SIR GLADYS	Quivering Meg? Mad Tom? I think on the whole I'd be safer kipping down in the stable with the Headless Horseman.
SPASM	(*shouts*) Quivering Meg? Where be ye? Mad Tom wants 'ee.
QUIVERING MEG (Betty Marsden)	(*husky*) Here I am, darling.
SPASM	I b'ain't as mad as I appear. Show the gen'lman to the —
ORCHESTRA	**DRAMATIC STING**
SPASM	— Tower Room.
QUIVERING MEG	(*horrified gasp*) No, Tom, no. Not the —
ORCHESTRA	**DRAMATIC STING**
QUIVERING MEG	— Tower Room.
SIR GLADYS	Why not the —
ORCHESTRA	**DRAMATIC STING**
SIR GLADYS	— Tower Room?
QUIVERING MEG	(*common*) Well, I haven't made the bed.
SPASM	Arr! Well in that case put him in the room where they bricked up the Black Nun in the fourteenth century. They do say you can hear her moaning to herself. Tis a wild unearthly sound — sort of like a medieval Debbie Reynolds. Still, she won't bother you if you don't bother her.
SIR GLADYS	Well I don't think I fancy that really. Haven't you got another room?
QUIVERING MEG	We have one other room — the Phantom Abbot's Room — it's got hot and cold running —
SIR GLADYS	Running what?
QUIVERING MEG	We don't know but you can feel them scampering over your face. The only trouble is that the Phantom Abbot's room is occupied.
SIR GLADYS	Who by?
SPASM	The Phantom Abbot. But you'll be alright because it's a double bed. He'll not take up much room. He keeps hisself to hisself. The only visitation you're likely to get is his phantom clammy feet in the small of your back.

SIR GLADYS	Isn't there anywhere else I can sleep?
SPASM	This isn't the Bodmin Hilton. You'll have to take pot luck with the Phantom Abbot. And if you want anything during the night — just scream.
ORCHESTRA	**SHORT LINK**
SIR GLADYS	As you may imagine I slept but fitfully that night. I was awakened at three a.m. by what sounded like the thudding of giant hooves and the champing of giant jaws outside my window. I slid quietly out of bed
Bill Pertwee	(as Karloff) While you're up Gladys — get me a glass of water, will you
SIR GLADYS	Certainly Abbot. I crossed to the window and there, in the forecourt of the hotel, was a huge shapeless grey creature with great bulging pink eyes and enormous whiskers. It was like a twenty-foot high Gerald Nabarro in a fur coat. The moon illuminated its ghastly face as pressed against the window pane and then, just as suddenly as it appeared, it vanished again. I was petrified. Sleep eluded me for the rest that night. After breakfast I decided to pay a call on an old friend of mi who lived in the neighbourhood — a certain Brigadier Grope-Mainwaring, the eminent big-game hunter and amateur taxidermist. His man, Grunter, answered the door.

F/X	**DOOR OPENS**
GRUNTER (Bill Pertwee)	(*cockney*) Well goodness me, sir — isn't it Sir Gladys Harbinger?
SIR GLADYS	Yes.
GRUNTER	Mother!
SIR GLADYS	But that's another story. Well Grunter, my good man, kindly take me to your master.
GRUNTER	Yes sir. This way sir, he's in the den stuffing a gorilla — up the chimney. Keeps the draught out.
F/X	**DOOR OPENS**
GRUNTER	Sir Gladys Harbinger to see you.
GROPE-MAINWARING (Hugh Paddick)	(*horsey*) Come in old boy. Good to see you. What brings you to these parts?
SIR GLADYS	Well, Grope-Mainwaring, you're something of an expert on strange phenomena. I saw something last night, so indescribably grisly that I never want to see anything like it again. Do you know what it is?
GROPE-MAINWARING	Mrs Thursday.
SIR GLADYS	A huge, grey, furry creature — with whiskers and big staring eyes.
GROPE-MAINWARING	Yes. Well you know when I was in East Africa the natives had a superstition about such a creature. They called it 'Umbolo M'gaga Umsapa Ligoli Putta putta futta futta n'gonga'. In English that means 'A twenty-foot high Gerald Nabarro in a fur coat'. But here? In Cornwall?
SIR GLADYS	I saw it last night, outside my bedroom window.
GROPE-MAINWARING	Of course I have heard rumours. I mean if one keeps one's ear to the ground, one does tend to get it full of mud and clinkers — among other things. All I can say is that if there's something strange going on in this neighbourhood, it emanates from that house on the hill. Come to this window here — use these binoculars — what do you see?
SIR GLADYS	Nothing.
GROPE-MAINWARING	You have to take them out of the case first.
SIR GLADYS	Ah yes. A house, with an outside chemical laboratory —
GROPE-MAINWARING	Yes — it belongs to a Professor Ludwig Von Nosepasture. He's engaged in experimental work for the government. Perhaps he can throw some light on the mystery.
ORCHESTRA	**SHORT LINK**
PROFESSOR (Kenneth Williams)	You wanted to see me?
SIR GLADYS	Yes, Professor.
PROFESSOR	Well come into the laboratory and close the door.
SIR GLADYS	What extraordinary equipment you have — curious test tubes — what strange retorts —

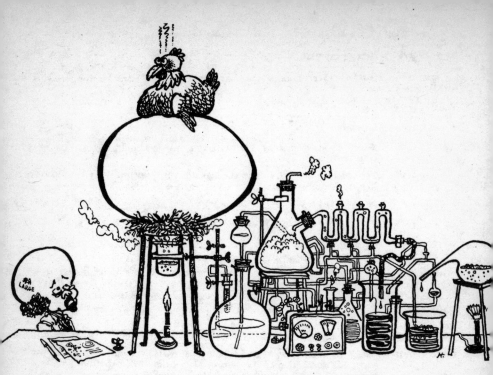

PROFESSOR	(*own voice*) Well I don't write the script ducky. (*professor*) But I can see you are curious about the nature of my work. I'm engaged in experiments to try and increase the world's food supply. As you can see, I am in the middle of an experiment with this chicken — you see, I've injected it with my new hormone preparation — and now observe — she's about to lay —
Hugh Paddick	(*chicken clucks*)
PROFESSOR	Come on girl.
F/X	**THUD**
SIR GLADYS	Good heavens. It's eight times the size of a normal egg.
PROFESSOR	Precisely. That's what I *call* going to work on an egg. Marvellous for the housewife — but not so good for the chicken. Look — here she goes again —
Hugh Paddick	(*painful squawks*)
SIR GLADYS	That's the first time I've ever seen a chicken go red in the face.
F/X	**THUD**
SIR GLADYS	Congratulations Professor. What other experiments are you working on
PROFESSOR	Well, foodwise I'm working on several. There's my project to cross a cow with a pig —
SIR GLADYS	What do you hope to get from that?

PROFESSOR	Veal and ham pie on the hoof. Also I'm working on a scheme to cross a pig with an armadillo — I'm going to call it a piggadillo —
SIR GLADYS	But won't it taste awful?
PROFESSOR	Sure, but just think of the crackling. But this is in the future. Right now I have just completed a very interesting experiment — I've produced a six-legged turkey — so that the whole family can have a drumstick. Look through the window — there they are, running about outside.
SIR GLADYS	Wonderful. When will they be on the market?
PROFESSOR	Just as soon as I can catch the swine. Mostly, though, I'm working on my hormone experiments to increase the size of animals. In this way we will be able to produce animals large . . . enough to . . .
F/X	**DOOR OPENS**
MISS LUST-TIPPET (Betty Marsden)	Professor, professor — the mouse has broken out of its cage and escaped.
SIR GLADYS	The mouse?
PROFESSOR	The one I was experimenting on. Quick — after him!
SIR GLADYS	Well surely a mouse can't do much harm.
MISS LUST-TIPPET	This one can. It's twenty-five feet high.
SIR GLADYS	Good heavens, that must be what I saw outside my window. A monster mouse — the mind boggles . . .
PROFESSOR	A twenty-five-feet high rogue mouse can be an ugly customer. Come on — we must follow its spoor —
SIR GLADYS	But surely a mouse doesn't leave spoor.
PROFESSOR	Well, whatever he leaves, we'll follow that.
ORCHESTRA	**DRAMATIC CHORD**
F/X	**GIGANTIC MOUSE CHEWING FOLIAGE**
MISS LUST-TIPPET	There he is — look — nibbling that oak tree. Good heavens, he must be nearly thirty foot tall by now.
PROFESSOR	We'll have to shoot it — hand me my gun.
SIR GLADYS	Which one?
PROFESSOR	The Mauser.
MISS LUST-TIPPET	(*panic*) It's seen us —
PROFESSOR	Stand your ground Miss Lust-Tippet — they can smell fear. It's going to charge.
Hugh Paddick	(*huge mouse trumpeting in rage*)
F/X	**THUDDING OF HOOVES APPROACHING**
SIR GLADYS	Don't shoot till you see the pink of its eyes.
PROFESSOR	Get behind that boulder. I'm going to let him have it.

F/X	**RIFLE SHOTS**
Hugh Paddick	(*huge mouse trumpeting in agony*)
PROFESSOR	Blast — I've only winged him. I got him in the leg.
F/X	**MOUSE LIMPING**
Hugh Paddick	(*huge mouse trumpeting in rage*)
MISS LUST-TIPPET	Look out, professor — look out.
SIR GLADYS	Good heavens — he's picked up the professor in his paws and —
PROFESSOR	(*screams*)
SIR GLADYS	Don't look Miss Lust-Tippet. It's not a pretty sight.
ORCHESTRA	**SHORT LINK**
SIR GLADYS	The giant mouse escaped but with only three good legs we knew it couldn't get far. Every grocer in Exeter was asked to co-operate and by dawn next day we had assembled four tons of gorgonzola cheese impregnated with a deadly poison. The mouse sniffed the cheese, took one nibble and —
Hugh Paddick	(*mouse expiring dramatically*)
F/X	**CREAKING AND THEN AN ENORMOUS THUD**
SIR GLADYS	The cheese had done its awful work. But unfortunately no one could get near enough to remove it and so it lies there to this day, four tons of slowly decomposing gorgonzola — not to mention a thirty-foot dead mouse! Oh well — I bet that'll help shift traffic on the Exeter By-Pass.
ORCHESTRA	**PLAY OFF**
	(*applause*)
Kenneth Horne	And now, here are the Fraser Hayes Four to sing a track from their new LP — The Golden Years of Lord Moran. The Fraser Hayes Four.
FRASER HAYES FOUR & ORCHESTRA	**MUSIC BREAK**
	(*applause*)
Kenneth Horne	Recently, Clarkson Rose, the Summer Show producer, celebrated his fiftieth anniversary in show business and many stars gathered to pay tribute to his long-running 'Twinkle'. This set me thinking. I thought, if Clarkie can do it, why not Hornie? So I took a lease on the Pier Pavilion at Bogmouth on Sylt and set about auditioning acts for my show —
ORCHESTRA	**MUSIC LINK**
	SEGUE INTO . . . . **REHEARSAL PIANO (SHEIKH OF ARABI IN FAST TWO)** **TAPS OVER**
Kenneth Horne	(*off mike*) Alright. Thank you dear, we'll let you know.
	MUSIC STOPS
Betty Marsden	(*common*) But Mr Horne, I haven't shown you my acro with the ferret.

Kenneth Horne	I think we can take the ferret as read. Keep in touch. Next please. Who's next?
GRUNTFUTTOCK (Kenneth Williams)	I am. J. Peasemold Gruntfuttock — England's Premier Yodelling Archbishop. A show in himself.
Kenneth Horne	Well, what is it you do?
GRUNTFUTTOCK	I perform feats of incredible dexterity and agility with a frankfurter sausage, a fire extinguisher and a goat, who unfortunately cannot be with us today, owing to prior engagements. However, as you are no doubt waiting eagerly to be enchanted by the full glory of my prowess, I shall demonstrate one of my facets, to whit and viz. — The Amazing Gruntfuttock — Escapologist Extraordinaire — assisted by the delectable Miss Exotica — *(shouts)* Buttercup, you're on.
BUTTERCUP (Betty Marsden)	Hello cheeky face.
GRUNTFUTTOCK	Excuse her appearance — she looks more exotic when she's got her teeth in. But her legs are good. Show the gentleman your legs.
Kenneth Horne	Er — no thanks. It's not really worth while her taking that boiler suit off. What actually is the nature of your act?
GRUNTFUTTOCK	Well I put her in a sack —
Kenneth Horne	That's understandable.
GRUNTFUTTOCK	Then I shall chain her up, won't I dear?
BUTTERCUP	Yes. Chains me up. When I'm in the sack.
GRUNTFUTTOCK	Yes. In the sack.
BUTTERCUP	In the sack. Yes.
GRUNTFUTTOCK	Then I throw her into an enormous tureen of flaming rancid chicken fat —
Kenneth Horne	So far I see nothing to object to.
GRUNTFUTTOCK	Then she escapes and joins me in the Grand Finale of the Act in which we sing 'Me and My Shadow'.
Kenneth Horne	And if she doesn't escape?
GRUNTFUTTOCK	I sing 'Me —'. I have another illusion which I will be glad to perform e.g. i.e. N.B. sawing the lady in half — Get in the box Buttercup.
Kenneth Horne	Are you sure you can do this?
GRUNTFUTTOCK	No. But I'll try anything once.
Kenneth Horne	Thank you Mr Gruntfuttock, but I don't really see you fitting into the show I had in mind.
GRUNTFUTTOCK	That's alright. Come on Buttercup, load the props on the barrow — we'll try Bernard Delfont — he's looking for a replacement for Barbra Streisand.
Kenneth Horne	Mmm. People who need people certainly don't need people like that. Next!
PANTO DAME (Bill Pertwee)	Sorry I'm late Mr 'Orne — I 'ad to 'oof it from Brixton.

Kenneth Horne	That's alright, Mrs er —
DAME	Mr. Mr Desmond Grapple. Panto Dame Specialities. My agent sent me up
Kenneth Horne	Hardly surprising. Well, what sort of experience have you?
DAME	I done all the pantos Mr 'Orne — I was an Ugly at Bolton last year and thi year I was going to be in Aladdin. I had me Twankey fixed but unfortunately it fell through.
Kenneth Horne	Never mind, it doesn't notice. Would you like to do your audition piec now?
DAME	Yes. I'll just give the pianist me parts. There you are dear — nice stead four and tacet for the patter.

(WITH PIANO)
'BESS OF THE A.T.S.'

I'm Bess, Bess,
Bess of the A.T.S.
Though sugar may be rationed
I'm the Sweetheart of the Mess —
(*breaks off*)
(*spoken*) Girls — how do you like me undies. I made 'em out of blackout curtains. Oh, but I've got a boy friend. He's a Free Pole — I think he's only going out with me to get his hands on my spam ration — Girls, girls — what about the meat ration. It's so small, I wrapped mine up in a bus ticket and it slipped through the punch-hole. Still, we won't let Hitler get us down — because —
(*sings*)
We may be short of nylons, of oranges and beer —
But the G.I.'s now have landed, so girls, let's give a cheer,
They're overpaid, they're oversexed, but at least they're over here.
Yes, I'm Bess, Bess —
Bess of the A.T.S.

There — Mr 'Orne — what do you think?

Kenneth Horne	Next please.
DAME	But you haven't seen me Winnie the WAAF . . .
Kenneth Horne	That's true. But if 1942 ever comes back I'll call you. Next.
DENTURES (Hugh Paddick)	Salutations. Allow me to present myself — The Great Omipaloni — th World's Fastest Illusionist — and also the dampest. Music maestro pleas — let the demonstration commence —
PIANO	**'IN THE SHADOWS' VERY SOFTLY AS BACKGROUND**
DENTURES	First — a few simple tricks — the quickness of the hand deceives the eye. Observe — a perfectly ordinary pocket handkerchief — I fold it thus, and thus —
Kenneth Horne	Then what happens?
DENTURES	I wipe my chin. Now I screw it into a ball and hey presto — (*music out*) — the flags of some nations.
Kenneth Horne	Some nations? Shouldn't that be *all* nations?

DENTURES	Ah yes. It should. But alas, I sent Somaliland, Schleswig-Holstein and Gallant Serbia to the laundry and they sent them back starched. And now can't get them up my sleeve. But to continue with this feat of prestidigitation — observe — I take this ordinary top hat, as you see, quite empty. I say the magic words — Sim Sala Bim — I place my hand inside and (*expression of disgust*) eugh! The rabbit seems to have died.
Kenneth Horne	What a pity.
DENTURES	Oh no matter. It takes care of supper. And so to the doves, observe as I produce doves from every part of my person — er — within reason, of course. How does he do it you ask?
Kenneth Horne	Well, no, actually. 'Why' was the question which sprang to mind.
DENTURES	Yes. You scoff, but observe — a dove — see, another dove, and another dove, and yet another —
F/X	**CAT MEOW**
DENTURES	Good gracious — a pussy cat — it's the doves that attract them you know. Still, the show must go on — see, another dove — well a handful of feathers — and, one moment, why what is this down my trousers?
ORCHESTRA	**DRUMS, CYMBAL CRASH**
DENTURES	A duck billed platypus.
Kenneth Horne	Very good. You amaze me.
DENTURES	Not as much as it amazes me. I had no idea it was there. Wait a second — what's this in my waistcoat pocket? A tortoise! Where did he come from? (*alarmed*) And what's this up my other sleeve? A cocker spaniel — good gracious. Will you forgive me, Mr Horne — I seem to be infested with livestock. Get down sir — down —
F/X	**DOG — WOOF WOOF**
DENTURES	— down I say (*going off*) bad dog — stop it!
Kenneth Horne	Next please. Good heavens, it's Rambling Syd Rumpo!
RAMBLING SYD	Hello me deario, chirrup a chirrup for the open road, for I boggle over hill and dale and dingle down in the forest-oh.
Kenneth Horne	Well, look out for the gin-traps. What brings you rambling into this audition? This is for a Summer Season at Bogmouth. I wouldn't have thought that was you at all.
RAMBLING SYD	Well, I bethought to meself — hey ho for the sea salt tang of the air, where the spume runs high and the seagulls wheel, and there's plenty of gash birds hanging about the promenade-oh.
Kenneth Horne	And what are you going to sing for us?
RAMBLING SYD	Well, I had a rummage in my ganderbag and I found an Irish bog-wanderer's song, which is sung by the itinerant peat-smoulderers as they huddle over their campfire smouldering their peat, which, of course can happen to anyone if they're not careful. And accounts for the fact that this is a sad song. It tells of a fair colleen by the name of Molly O'Rosenthal — who peddles her lummocks through

the streets of Dublin — it's a trade that's died out now on account of the tourists . . .
And she sings as she trundles her cart from door to door this plaintive lament —

GUITAR ACCOMPANIMENT

(*sadly*)
I have fine lummocks
Fine lummocks have I
Too-ra-loo-ra too-ra-lay
Who my fine lummocks, fine lummocks will buy —
Bite them, you'll find that they're fresh caught today.
Ooooooooooooh —

(*brightly*)
Tiddly-eye-tye-tye
Tiddlyboodle-um a doodle-um
Tiddly-eye-tye; they're the fairest ever seen.
Tiddly-eye-tye-tye
Tiddly fumble in me rumble-um
And who will bite the lummock of a fair colleen?

(*guitar repeats melody of last line while Rambling Syd makes appropriate whooping noises*)

Kenneth Horne	Thank you Rambling Syd and R.I.P.
RAMBLING SYD	Pardon?
Kenneth Horne	Just wishful thinking. Next. Who are you dear?
SUNNY MOLESTRANGLER (Betty Marsden)	(*coming on*) (*very old*) Sunny Molestrangler, V.A.F.
Kenneth Horne	Is that your name or a description of your act? What do you actually do?
SUNNY	I am billed as Barnsley's Shirley Temple. Miss Vitality-plus.
Kenneth Horne	Well, would you like to give us a sample of your work?
SUNNY	I beg your pardon? You'll have to speak up, dear. You see, I don't wear the appliance when I'm working. The batteries make an unsightly bulge in my tu-tu. But I'll give you a sample of my work if you like. Could you direct me towards the microphone? You see, I don't wear my glasses on stage — it cuts down my sex appeal. Is this the microphone? Would this be it?
Kenneth Horne	Here you are. But I thought you old-timers didn't need a microphone.
SUNNY	Oh I don't need it to sing into. It's for holding meself up. I'm a little short of breath these days. Right — a-one, a-two —

(*sings with piano accompaniment*)

I'm young and healthy — and I've got — er — er — er — er (*pause — then snores*)

Kenneth Horne	Good heavens she's fallen asleep. Wake up dear, you're on.
SUNNY	(*startled*) Oh — er — into the dance.
PIANO	**'MOONLIGHT BAY' VERY SLOW. WITH EVEN SLOWER TAPS.**

SUNNY	(*heavy breathing during breaks*)
Kenneth Horne	Alright — thank you dear.
SUNNY	Well, what did you think Mr Horne?
Kenneth Horne	It's not quite what I'm looking for.
SUNNY	I'm sorry I muffed the cartwheel.
Kenneth Horne	Yes, well it's not easy in a bathchair. Next please. Oh hello, haven't we met before?
JULIAN (Hugh Paddick)	Yes. I'm Julian and this is my friend, Sandy.
Kenneth Horne	Well, what brings you trolling in here?
SANDY (Kenneth Williams)	Well, ducky, we heard you was doing auditions and we thought you'd be interested in having a vada at our spesh.
Kenneth Horne	Well, I should be delighted to have a vada. What do you actually do?
SANDY	We do a bit of everything, don't we Jule?
JULIAN	Oh yes we have many facets. You have your Sandy and Jule, the Bona Brothers — twenty tiny toes tapping their way to the top. Or we can do amazing feats on the trampoline.
Kenneth Horne	I'm sure you can.
SANDY	Make your hair stand on end we could. But now we'd like to present the Bewildering Julian and Co. I'm Co. We do telepathy. Right — get your turban on Jule.
JULIAN	There. How does it look?
Kenneth Horne	Very striking. But should it have wax fruit on the top?
JULIAN	Right Sand. Pass among Mr Horne and borrow from him any ordinary object such as a bus ticket, and I will bewilder him by telling him what it is.
SANDY	Have you such an object as a bus ticket about your person, Mr Horne?
Kenneth Horne	Wait a minute. Yes. There you are.
SANDY	Thank you. Now then Jule — are you ready to bewilder him?
JULIAN	Nearly. I'm going into me trance first. Ooh — aah — ooh — that's it. The mystic forces are occupying me.
SANDY	They're occupying him. There, see. He is actually occupied now. You can't get through to him when he's like that. Sometimes he's occupied for days. Are you ready?
JULIAN	I am ready.
SANDY	Then tell me — what am I holding in my hand?
JULIAN	Wait a moment — it's coming through. I can feel the waves.
SANDY	It's coming over him in waves now.
JULIAN	I've got it. Is it a potato shaped like Lloyd George's knee?

SANDY	No, but you're near.
JULIAN	Is it a Shepherd's Pie?
SANDY	Er — it is oblong and it has numbers on it.
JULIAN	An oblong shepherd's pie with numbers on it.
Kenneth Horne	Don't you think we ought to give him a clue?
SANDY	(*shouts*) Now what am I holding, now don't miss the bus, come on, that's the ticket.
JULIAN	Bus? Ticket?
SANDY	Fantabulosa! It is, as you see — a bus ticket. Doesn't that amaze you Mr Horne. The way he got it.
Kenneth Horne	Fantastic. But I must be honest — I would have been rather more impressed if he'd been wearing a blindfold.
SANDY	Oh we've tried that. It's hopeless.
ORCHESTRA	**PLAY OFF MUSIC**
Kenneth Horne	And they say Variety is coming back. Well, if it's anything like that, I shall lock myself in the bathroom until it goes away again. Well, that's it for this week, except to say that if you have any suggestions or complaints why don't you put them on a postcard and address them to — Mr Justin Tramwicket, The Lighthouse, Nuneaton. He won't be able to help you, but he'd appreciate a postcard. Nobody ever writes to him. Cheerio. See you next week.
	(*applause*)
ORCHESTRA	**'ROUND THE HORNE' PLAY OUT**

ROUND THE HORNE

2ND SERIES — PROGRAMME NO. 12
TRANSMISSION: Sunday 29th May 1966:
1.30-2.00 p.m. LIGHT PROGRAMME

Hugh Paddick	My lords, ladies and gentlemen, Barmitzvah boy, father of the groom, mother of twins, bride of the gorilla, lord of the flies, lion of Judah and Toad of Toad Hall. Your President, His Highness, the Viceroy of the Balls Pond Road, wishes to take metal polish strained through a sock with all his honoured guests. Please be upstanding and charge your socks. The Toast is a better, fuller life with celluloid underwear, with which I would like to couple 'Round The Horne'.
ORCHESTRA	**SIGNATURE TUNE**
Douglas Smith	And in this edition our special guests are — The Revolting Muldoons and Bobo — in a despicable act with a bread pudding, Professor Eli Neckstrap and Trixie — exploding a goat for *you* — there'll be a trip round the world in song with Sherpa Gutbucket and the electric Druids, there'll be a laugh or two from your cheerful chin-up boy, the Reverend Peeping Tom Codpiece — the juggling theosophist, and compering the proceedings is your own, your very own, Kenneth 'I won't unscrew my elbows, I'm not stopping' Horne —
ORCHESTRA	**MUSIC**
Kenneth Horne	That was Douglas Smith — a suitable case for treatment — Is there a Vet in the house? Well now here are the answers to last week's questions. The First Aid question — well, the answer came in several parts, as follows. You squeeze it, you hold it under a cold tap till it goes down, you smear it with wintergreen, and then you leap about screaming — that's not laid down in the text book, but it's almost inevitable if you smear it with wintergreen. Now from rheumatism to the final part of the question — well you'll remember I showed you a picture and asked — 'What were they doing?' Well, he was administering the kiss of life. Mr Gruntfuttock what can I say? I try to be patient with you but this time you really have let your imagination run riot. Even if what you had suggested was remotely conceivable I'm sure the International Red Cross would have stepped in long ago. Not to mention Interpol. Smith — make the announcement.
Douglas Smith	Lo, I come from haunts of coot and fern — well Kings Road actually. So to be factual, it's just a coot. In a cowslip's bell I lie — I can put a girdle round the earth in forty minutes *and* make it five pounds lighter —
Kenneth Horne	Smith!
Douglas Smith	Thanks to Dobbitex medical cummerbunds for horses — They said I was mad — they said Mozart was mad, but I'll show you, I'll show you all — you see this ray-gun I'm holding in my hand — unless you give me the secret plans, I'll —
F/X	**WHOOSH**
Kenneth Williams	(*deep-voiced American*) Not so fast Doctor Krautmeyer — Stand back Mr Horne —
Kenneth Horne	Good heavens — it's Batman!
Kenneth Williams	(*deep-voiced American*) Yes, Mr President, wherever the forces of evil strike, Batman is there. (*own voice*) How do you like me tights, ducky?
Kenneth Horne	They suit you!
Kenneth Williams	Ta. (*deep-voiced American*) Alright, Robin —
Hugh Paddick	(*shy voice*) Yes, Batman. What do you want me to do?

Kenneth Williams	(*deep-voiced American*) Grab this power crazed maniac and take him to a place where he can do no harm. (*Douglas protests as Hugh leads him off*). And so perish all enemies of democracy. America is on the march. That government of the people, by the people and for the people shall not perish from the Earth. (*own voice*) Except when it's expedient. (*character voice*) If you're ever in trouble Mr President — just send for Batman.
F/X	**WHOOSH AS HE TAKES OFF**
Kenneth Williams	I never get this trouble on Twenty Questions. Oh well, now it's time for the Kenneth Horne Theatre of Suspense.
GRAMS	**ELECTRONIC MUSIC**
Hugh Paddick	There is a strange creature that lurks in your libido. Some call it fear, some have another name for it — they call it (*chuckles*) Mr Podmore, the Lodger. Be it fear, *or* be it Mr Podmore the Lodger, it only comes out at night and prowls around the Twilight (*echo on*) Sanctum-um-um-um.
GRAMS	**ELECTRONIC MUSIC**
DR POSTERN (Kenneth Horne)	My name is Dr Postern, nee Bulstrode, but we won't go into that. Suffice to say that it didn't work out and I was discharged from the Indian Army, and the yak had its licence endorsed. When I returned to London from campaigning in the Khyber, I was at a loose end. Picture me if you will, as I was then, in the Spring of 1888 — a portly red-faced man with mutton-chop whiskers, a shepherds-pie beard and a shock of red hair — the shock being that it used to revolve and squirt water. I took chambers in Baker Street with a private investigator — a hawk-faced man with a hook nose, from which depended a carcass of beef. His dress too tended to the flamboyant — he affected a Sherlock Holmes hat, a Sherlock Holmes cape and smoked a Sherlock Holmes pipe. His name, dear listener, as you have probably guessed was Gladys Lustgirdle, a pseudonym which fools nobody, except, we hope, the executors of the late Arthur Conan Doyle. One afternoon, I was in his study while he was working on a case — and, as was his wont, to help his concentration he was playing a wistful air on his instrument —
ORCHESTRA	**SOLO TROMBONE — 'ORYS CREOLE TROMBONE'**
GLADYS LUSTGIRDLE (Kenneth Williams)	Well, Dr Postern, dear old friend — I think I've cracked it.
DR POSTERN	Oh bad luck. I'll put a plaster on it.
GLADYS LUSTGIRDLE	No, my dear old friend, companion in adversity, trusty helpmeet, and king-sized twit — I was referring to the case — The Curious Incident of the Tap Dancing Ferret Nobbler. Sir Redvers Cornposture was trying to put us off the scent — it was Lady McHorsetrouser all the time.
DR POSTERN	Incredible, Gladys — your powers of deduction never cease to amaze me. How do you know?
GLADYS LUSTGIRDLE	(*very fast — almost without punctuations*) Elementary, my dear Postern — you see, Leonide Grasspepper posed as Otto Von Potroast in order to confuse her husband Sylvia Mousehabit. Pinochle and Marks were in league with Rabbi McWhirter — the upholsterer's dog gave the game away, when Daphne Lobes and Lord Pubetrumpet traced the smell to Limbo Charlie's Fried Halibut Den in Tunbridge Wells. The rest you know. What do you say to that Postern?
DR POSTERN	(*snores*)

F/X	**KNOCK ON DOOR**
GLADYS LUSTGIRDLE	Ah that'll be faithful old Mrs Houston — she who has served me well these many years — also my housekeeper. Come in faithful old Mrs Houston.
F/X	**DOOR OPENS**
MRS HOUSTON (Hugh Paddick)	(*gruff*) Here's your tea Mister Gladys. Where shall I put the tray?
DR POSTERN	Answers please on a postcard to the Head of Light Entertainment, BBC — Ghana.
MRS HOUSTON	There's a lady downstairs, says she's the Countess of Scoon —
GLADYS LUSTGIRDLE	Well, send her up immediately.
MRS HOUSTON	Certainly sir.
F/X	**FOOTSTEPS RETREATING AND RETURNING**
MRS HOUSTON	The Countess of Scoon.
COUNTESS OF SCOON (Betty Marsden)	(*distraught*) Mr Lustgirdle — I had to come and see you, sob, sob, gulp gasp, it's my gulp, husband, he's gasp, sob, disappeared, sob, gasp.
GLADYS LUSTGIRDLE	He's, sharp intake of breath, what?
COUNTESS	Sob, gulp, disappeared. What's the gulp, matter, have you got sob, gasp cloth, gulp, ears?
GLADYS LUSTGIRDLE	What do you make of that Dr Postern?
DR POSTERN	(*snores*)
Kenneth Williams	(*own voice*) Prod him with your ducks head umbrella dear or we'll never get on.
DR POSTERN	(*waking startled*) What? what? Er — take your clothes off, Madam and I'll examine you.
COUNTESS	I beg your pardon?
GLADYS LUSTGIRDLE	She's my customer, Doctor, not yours.
DR POSTERN	I know. But it sometimes works.
GLADYS LUSTGIRDLE	Now calm yourself, dear lady. Tell me the whole story —
COUNTESS	Well, gulp, my sob, sob, husband, gasp —
Kenneth Williams	(*own voice*) I think you can drop that love. I think you've squeezed the last titter out of that bit.
COUNTESS	He went out to buy a newspaper and . . . hasn't come back yet.
DR POSTERN	When did he go?
COUNTESS	Twenty-five years ago. April the Fourth 1863.
GLADYS LUSTGIRDLE	Then we haven't got a moment to lose. April the Fourth 1863 — that's the day we're looking for. If we find that day we've got our man.

DR POSTERN	But how will you tackle it?
GLADYS LUSTGIRDLE	I shall disguise myself as April the Fifth 1863 and hang about outside. In the meanwhile, I shall leave the Countess in your care.
DR POSTERN	And with that, Gladys clapped on his deerstalker hat, clapped on his ferretstalker boots and clapped on the offbeat as he shuffled off to Buffalo —
COUNTESS	Oh Doctor Postern — I'm afraid for my husband.
DR POSTERN	Surely he's old enough to be afraid for himself. Have you any clue to his whereabouts?
COUNTESS	Nothing at all. Except this note he left pinned to the cat in the fridge — it says — 'Dear Lil — have gone to Number 14 Seaview Terrace, East India Dock Road — will not be coming back ever, so don't wait up''.
DR POSTERN	Hmm. Not much to go on. Still, we can try that address. And the sooner, the better.
COUNTESS	Good. I've got a hansom outside.
DR POSTERN	Pausing only long enough for the double entendre contained in the last line to sink in, I hurried her to the street.
F/X	**CLIP CLOP OF HOOVES**
COUNTESS	Ho there cabbie — you, driving the coconut shells —

Bill Pertwee	Did you call me madam?
COUNTESS	No, but I will if you prefer it — ho there madam — do you know Limehouse?
Bill Pertwee	No, but if you hum a few bars, I'll soon pick it up.
DR POSTERN	Isn't that rather an old joke?
Bill Pertwee	Not really. After all, this is 1888 — what do you expect, David Frost?
DR POSTERN	No. That is one thing in its favour. Well then, whip up the mare and drive to 14 Seaview Terrace.
Bill Pertwee	Right sir. Hi-ho Solly.
F/X	**GALLOPING HOOVES OFF INTO DISTANCE**
	(*pause*)
DR POSTERN	He might have waited for us.
ORCHESTRA	**MUSIC LINK ENDING ON CHINESE NOTE**
DR POSTERN	That evening found us in the narrow winding streets of Limehouse — around us thronged the inscrutable inhabitants of London's Chinatown chattering in their inscrutable native tongue.
OMNES	**BABBLE IN UNISON 'LHUBARB LHUBARB'**
DR POSTERN	Thank you — thank you — we'll let you know.
	(*babble subsides*)
COUNTESS	Where are we Doctor Postern? I think we're lost.
DR POSTERN	I'll just enquire — excuse me — can you direct me to 14 Seaview Terrace
Hugh Paddick	(*Chinese*) Ah so. Have honour to be of assistance to distinguished stranger in neighbourhood. First right at Celestial all night Bagwash, continue to Pie and Eel shop of Seven Dragons, turn left at offices of Honourable Kosher Horsemeat Authority, and you can't miss it — may good fortune attend your journey and may many children spring forth from your loins —
DR POSTERN	Thank you constable.
Hugh Paddick	A pleasure. Mind how you go.
GRAMS	**SHORT LINK**
F/X	**FOOTSTEPS ON PAVEMENT. THEY COME TO A STOP.**
COUNTESS	That must be it. That cafe.
DR POSTERN	Good heavens — look what's written on the window. 'The Moo-Cow-a-Go-Go Opium Den. Proprietor Fu Manchu'. You go and get the police — I'll go and beard the sinister doctor in his den — and if that doesn't work I'll moustache him in the bathroom.
COUNTESS	Be careful Doctor Postern — here, you'd better take this —
DR POSTERN	What is it?

COUNTESS	A bottle of Bicarbonate of Soda. There's enough in there to blow us all to kingdom come. Goodbye, good luck.
DR POSTERN	I strode purposefully down the stairs, into a smoke filled cellar. In bunks all around the walls lay victims of the dreadful habit. As I passed a bunk, its occupant stirred fitfully and croaked out —
Bill Pertwee	Oi baldy! Shut the door will ya?
DR POSTERN	I looked around. So these were the slaves of the dreaded poppy. An old crone shambled towards me offering me her wares —
Betty Marsden	(*old crone*) Hello dearie — like to buy a dreaded poppy?
DR POSTERN	I didn't know it was dreaded Poppy Day. She threw back her head and gave an awful cackle.
Betty Marsden	(*horrible cackle*)
DR POSTERN	That was a pretty awful cackle —
Betty Marsden	(*own voice*) Well it was a pretty awful joke. (*old crone*) We have been expecting you Doctor Postern — through here —
F/X	**TINKLE OF BEADED CURTAIN**
DR POSTERN	I pushed my way through a beaded curtain and found myself in a huge, gleaming laboratory. So this was Fu Manchu's den. The sinister Doctor stood with his back to me, bent over a figure strapped to a table, about to inject it with a hypodermic syringe — at least that's what I think he was doing, but in the dim light it might well have been a bicycle pump, in which case I'd sooner *not* know what he was up to. He turned, and in a sudden flash, I recognised my old adversary —
CHOU EN GINSBERG (Kenneth Williams)	Ah Mr Horne — we meet again.
DR POSTERN	You? Fu Manchu?
CHOU EN GINSBERG	Not exactly. Fu Manchu-en-Ginsberg. Welcome return of old favourite — cue for applause —
	(*applause*)
CHOU EN GINSBERG	Thank you. You are so kind. You've made an old fiendish master mind very happy. (*sings*) Solly, Solly, don't ever wander away from the Olly and me (*breaks off*). Yes — it is I — me hisself.
DR POSTERN	But why have you dropped the Ginsberg?
CHOU EN GINSBERG	Made me sound too foreign. In China that is. Ahah, I see by explession on your face that you lecognise cleature stlapped to opelating table —
DR POSTERN	It's the Earl of Scoon.
CHOU EN GINSBERG	Collection. *Was* Earl of Scloon. Became slave of ploppy and is now in my plower.
DR POSTERN	Plower?
CHOU EN GINSBERG	As in plower-game. But now you know my seclet, you die — ahah — ahah — ahah — oho — eehee — ahaha — ohoho — tee-hee — hoho — or even tee-ho. But before you die — a little entertainment — will summon

loveliest of all my concubines, most ~~fragile flower~~ of the East, Lotus
Blossom —

F/X	**GONG**
LOTUS BLOSSOM (Hugh Paddick)	Yers, oh mighty mandarin, oh great warlord, in whose presence all bow down and quail. What do you want, mate?
CHOU EN GINSBERG	Ah my little lychee nut — (*own voice*) You're not seeing her at her best today — (*Chou*) Come my darling — we would have some music.
LOTUS BLOSSOM	Certainly, oh celestial radiance, cock. Would you like me to strum a wistful air?
DR POSTERN	I wouldn't mind. Which one?
LOTUS BLOSSOM	The one growing out me ear. Or shall I seduce your ear with sweet nightingale tones, as if you had strayed into an enchanted grotto — or would you like me to shake it abaht a bit?
Kenneth Williams	(*own voice*) When she's had a few beers she's as common as muck. (*Chou*) Sing for us — after two — A-one, A-two —

LOTUS BLOSSOM	(*sings — as in 'Gypsy'*) Let me entertain you and we'll have a real good time, yes sir, we'll have a —
OU EN GINSBERG	Yes. Alright darling. Leave your name at the stage door of the Hippodrome — Bulawayo. Now, my fliend, you will excuse me — I have expeliment to perform. I am about to plunge this sylinge into the Earl of Scoon's arm — when he awakes — he will be a mindless lobot.
DR POSTERN	Not so fast — you see this fifteen-inch naval gun I'm holding — one false move and I shall fire a fifteen-inch navel at you.
OU EN GINSBERG	Too late — aha! See — it is done. But you will never take me alive.
DR POSTERN	Antl with that, the evil doctor leapt from the window with a cry of —
OU EN GINSBERG	Aaaaaaaah — ugh!
DR POSTERN	And landed in a passing concrete mixer. He was later laid by Queen Victoria as the foundation stone of the Lady Birdstrangler Home for Methylated Spirit Drinkers. And what of the erstwhile Earl of Scoon? It was too late to save him. When he awoke he had become a mindless robot, almost incapable of intelligent speech — all he could say was —

| SEAMUS ANDROID (Bill Pertwee) | Hello and welcome to the Seamus Android Show. |

ORCHESTRA   **PLAY OFF**

(*applause*)

Kenneth Horne   What a tragic end for anyone. And now the Fraser Hayes Four, the clos[e] harmony group who are said to have perfect pitch — it's the one outside the saloon bar of the Baboon and Trumpet. Ladies and Gentlemen — The Fraser Hayes Four.

(*applause*)

FRASER HAYES FOUR & ORCHESTRA   **MUSIC BREAK**

(*applause*)

Douglas Smith   And now — Trends.

ORCHESTRA   **MUSIC 'TRENDS'**

Kenneth Horne   First — fashion — Celia Twick reports from Paris.

CELIA TWICK (Betty Marsden)   What is Pierre Balmain up to behind the closed doors of his Paris Salon?

Kenneth Williams   (*French*) Mind your own business, ducky. I don't ask you how you spend your time.

Kenneth Horne   The British male is becoming more and more clothes conscious. The trend has even reached the Police Force, who, we hear, are having new with-i[t] uniforms designed for them. Over now to the cocktail bar at Bow Street Magistrates Court, where top designers are exhibiting what tomorrow's policemen will be wearing.
The parade is described by the fashion correspondents of the Police Gazette — Inspector Tom Grutt and Detective Sergeant Obadiah Grasspole.

GRAMS	**TINKLING COCKTAIL MUSIC UNDER**
TOM GRUTT (Bill Pertwee)	*(gruff cockney)* Evening all. First we see Roger and George chatting at the bar — Roger wears the basic little black outfit that no trendy copper on the beat should be without. Gone the cumbersome helmet and in its place a cheeky tomboyish little number in pink velour with a bobble on top — what fun! Above the peep toed Courrege boots, white PVC, of course, he wears Bermuda Shorts, cut daringly low over the hips, to reveal just a hint of midriff. Well done Roger — you look stunning.
GRAMS	**CHA CHA — UP AND OUT FOR DIALOGUE**
TOM GRUTT	*(gruff cockney)* George has gone gay in a figure hugging pastel one-piece cat suit. How ideal for those interminable peace marches. Gone the bulky pockets of yesteryear — whistle, notebook and truncheon are carried in a dinky handbag. Look out Mr Burglar — George is ready for anything.
GRAMS	**'A PRETTY GIRL IS LIKE A MELODY'**

<table>
<tr><td>GRASSPOLE
(Hugh Paddick)</td><td>For evening wear, Sydney has really gone to town. Notice his non-crush black velvet matador pants, fastened at the knee with a simple rhinestone buckle — so practical for those draughty rides in a Black Maria — his frilled shirt surmounted by a shortie op-art cape in wild silk — and should it come on rain, why, no matter — see — it is reversible. The Alsatian on the leash is option and can be dyed to match the colour of your hair. But just so that we do not forg that Rover too is in the force, his toenails are painted regulation grey. Thank you Sydney, and stop it Rover. Yes — it's oo la la in the Police Force of tomorrow. Carry on constable.</td></tr>
<tr><td>GRAMS</td><td>MUSIC UP AND OUT.</td></tr>
<tr><td>Kenneth Horne</td><td>If that's the uniformed branch I can't wait to see the plain clothes. Next, trends in music. Now, when I say the name Rambling Syd Rumpo — what does it evoke? Well, unfortunately it always seems to evoke Rambling Syd Rumpo — and here he is.</td></tr>
<tr><td>RAMBLING SYD
(Kenneth Williams)</td><td>Hello me deario, for I'll haul away me najjer till the groatbender comes oh.</td></tr>
<tr><td>Kenneth Horne</td><td>Yes, try and hold out till then. You see, it makes such a deafening noise, and people might be having their lunch. And what are you going to sing for us this week?</td></tr>
<tr><td>RAMBLING SYD</td><td>Well, I've been dipping in me ganderbag to find you a gladsome ditty and I've come up with a very tender and furtive madrigal, which has been passed down from Father to son, until the handle dropped off. Tis an old Sussex courting song and tells the story of a young swain who stands beneath his loved one's bower — he's a very small swain, but then she's got a very low bower. It's the prevailing winds, you see. Anyway he stands there in the full moonlight a'plighting his troth. It's best to plight it where you can see it, otherwise you're liable to make a dog's breakfast of the whole rigmarole. So the he is — plighting his troth.</td></tr>
</table>

PLIGHTING HIS TROTH

Kenneth Horne	I've often wondered — what is a troth?
RAMBLING SYD	It's a small furry creature, with fins — it's a cross between a trout and a sloth.
Kenneth Horne	A curious match.
RAMBLING SYD	Yes, I often wonder what they saw in each other in the first place. Although I suppose the sloth hanging upside down tends to have a different slant on things. Anyway, nowadays people say that they're extinct, but I believe they're hanging about somewhere and they'll come round when they're hungry.
Kenneth Horne	Anyway — they obviously have to be plighted.
RAMBLING SYD	Only in the hot weather. They go off otherwise. So, anyway, this lover is under this tree singing to his light of love — (*guitar vamp*) and he tells her of his love as follows —

GUITAR ACCOMPANIMENT

Will you still love me Mary-oh
When my grussets be bended low
When my orbs grow dim and my splod grows white
And my cordwangle makes an ugly sight
And my grussets be bended low-oh
My grussets be bended low.

(*spoken*) And she sings back to him —

(*sings*)

You ask me if I'll love you-oh
Though your grussets be bended low
Though your orbs are dim and your splod be white
And your cordwangle makes an ugly sight
If I'll feel the way I do tonight
My answer will still beeeeeeeeeee-no!

(*applause*)

Kenneth Horne	Thank you Rambling Syd. Well, the nostalgia for the Forties is still with us. People are getting sentimental over the period when Jack Warner was minding his bike and not 'how you go'. When Peter Cook and Dudley Moore were known as Enoch and Ramsbotham, when Lord Moran was only writing prescriptions, when Danny la Rue was Doris Hare, when Quintin Hogg was only a piglet, and Harold Wilson was still with Keppel and Betty. And here is an excerpt from one of those wonderful wartime films starring Dame Celia Molestrangler and ageing juvenile Binkie Huckaback.
GRAMS	'WHITE CLIFFS OF DOVER'
ᵢIA MOLESTRANGLER (Betty Marsden)	Oh Charles — what's happened to us?
BINKIE HUCKABACK (Hugh Paddick)	Happened? To us?
CELIA	Yes. Happened. You've changed.
BINKIE	A man must change. After all, it's been five years Fiona. A man can't wear the same vest forever.

CELIA	It's more than that.
BINKIE	Yes. My socks as well.
CELIA	How easy it is for you to be flippant. Oh Charles, you take a woman heart in your hands and trample on it. Once we had something that beautiful and fine. Don't you feel anything any more?
BINKIE	I still feel the way I used to. It's just that you don't notice it any mor
CELIA	Oh Charles — a woman needs certain things. She needs to be loved, wanted, cherished, sought after, wooed, flattered, cossetted, pampered She needs sympathy, affection, devotion, understanding, tenderness, infatuation, adulation, idolatry — that isn't much to ask Charles.
BINKIE	I know.
CELIA	I know you know.
BINKIE	I know you know I know.
CELIA	I know. Then why can't you give it to me?
BINKIE	It's not easy Fiona.
CELIA	It's not hard Charles. If you try. And now you're going.
BINKIE	I have to. This is something I should have done a long time ago.
CELIA	Is it *her*? Daphne?
BINKIE	Yes Fiona. I must go. She needs me.
CELIA	I need you. Does that mean nothing?
BINKIE	Daphne needs me more. Much more. But I shall think of you all the ti I'm with her.
CELIA	I'll wait for you Charles. You will come back to me won't you? Please you'll come back to me.
BINKIE	I always come back don't I?
CELIA	Oh Charles — when will you come back? How long will it be this ti
BINKIE	That depends on Daphne. Perhaps five minutes —perhaps ten. Good Fiona —
CELIA	Goodbye Charles.
BINKIE	(*shouts*) Come along Daphne — walkies —
Bill Pertwee	(*dog barking*)
ORCHESTRA	**MUSIC LINK**
	(*applause*)
Kenneth Horne	Oh how that took me back — to last Sunday when I saw it on televisio Now everybody who considers themselves to be a really trendy person nowadays has a publicity man. So I thought I'd get myself one. I went to firm which specialises in publicising show business people. The sign the door said 'Bona Relations'.
F/X	**DOOR OPENS**

Kenneth Horne	Hello — is anybody there?
JULIAN (Hugh Paddick)	Hello — I'm Julian and this is my friend, Sandy.
SANDY (Kenneth Williams)	How bona to vada your dolly old eek again Mr Horne. What brings you trolling in here?
Kenneth Horne	Well I felt that I was badly in need of some Public Relations.
SANDY	Well chacun à son goût — that's your actual French you know.
Kenneth Horne	No, you see I want to become a celebrity and I thought you could help me.
JULIAN	Well, of course, in the field of public relations we have handled them all.
SANDY	Handled 'em all we have. In the public relations field. Right, first of all, we must consider your image. How should we project him, do you think Jule?
JULIAN	I don't know. I've been wondering that myself. Well now, let's see. You don't have any talents do you? You don't sing or act or dance or nothing?
Kenneth Horne	Well I was once runner up in the Sydenham Palais all-comers free-style paso-doble. I got a jar of boiled sweets for that. Course that was in 1926. I've eaten most of them now.
SANDY	Yes. Well there's not really enough to build a career on in that. What you want to be is your actual TV personality. That means you can't do nothing but you make a fortune sitting on panels talking about it.
JULIAN	Now if we're going to make you a celebrity, people have got to be intrigued by you — they've got to wonder about you. Take Sean Connery — we all wonder about Sean Connery don't we?
SANDY	Oh yes. We all wonder about him alright. Is he or isn't he? We ask ourselves.
Kenneth Horne	Is he or isn't he what?
SANDY	Nobody knows ducky. If we did, we wouldn't wonder. You have to become a figure of mystery and romance in all the gossip columns — you know the sort of thing — 'Who is rumoured to be that way about Kenneth Horne?' or 'Kenneth Horne walks out of Casino Royale'.
Kenneth Horne	But I'm not even in the film.
SANDY	That should simplify it.
JULIAN	I've got it. We link his name with a well-known film star. How about 'Kenneth Horne rumoured to be marrying Frank Sinatra'. That'd make him talked about.
SANDY	No ducky, *not* a good idea. I mean it's alright for Mia Farrow, she's more his type. Besides we used the story last week for Robertson Hare.
JULIAN	Course we'll have to change your name — I mean you can't get anywhere with a name like Kenneth Horne. No, you want something more butch — something forceful — like Ruff Trade or Surge Thrust — or Marlon Twist.
Kenneth Horne	Marlon Twist?

SANDY	Yes, ducky. Marlon Twist. It's you, it's you! Then you have to be see about the place — getting drunk in nightclubs, assaulting the police inviting the Prime Minister to breakfast — you've got to have your public exposure. Get your exposure right.
Kenneth Horne	How do I do that?
JULIAN	Well, you have to be seen at all the openings. Get your openings lined 'Kenneth Horne photographed at World Premiere squiring Ursula Andress.'
Kenneth Horne	But I don't know her.
SANDY	That's where we come in. We can fix that up with the studios. Of course, it costs a bit. For two hundred guineas you can go with Samar Eggar — for a hundred you can go with Monica Vitti.
Kenneth Horne	I didn't want to go that high. I didn't really want to spend more tha twenty pounds.
SANDY	Well I think we can fix you up, don't you Jule?
JULIAN	Yes. For twenty quid we can get you Mrs Shufflewick.
ORCHESTRA	**PLAY OFF**
	(*applause*)
Kenneth Horne	Well, I took up their suggestion. I'm changing my whole image and course, my name. So that brings us to the end of another edition of 'Round The Twist'. Cheerio. See you next week.
	(*applause*)
ORCHESTRA	**'ROUND THE HORNE' PLAY OUT**

ROUND THE HORNE

3RD SERIES — PROGRAMME NO. 7
TRANSMISSION : Sunday 26th March 1967 :
1.30-2.00 p.m. LIGHT PROGRAMME

GRAMS	**'GOING FOR A SONG' MUSIC**
Douglas Smith	Now here is the first antique that we're asking our panel to value. P[?] what do you make of this?
PLINT (Kenneth Williams)	Well I've never seen one like this before. I would say it was a Byzantine combine harvester — or an ancient Egyptian water buffalo of the typ[?] used as a back scratcher.
Douglas Smith	Lady Duckhawker?
LADY DUCKHAWKER (Betty Marsden)	It's exquisite. I *have* seen one of these before, in fact I have a pair of th[?] at home. It is, in fact, a Chippendale cheese fork or vest puncturer.
Douglas Smith	Loam?
LOAM (Bill Pertwee)	You're both wrong. It's a loomers jar, late nineteenth century, and it w[?] used at Queen Victoria's Jubilee for coddling wasps — or badgers. Wa[?] or badgers — nineteenth century.
Douglas Smith	Hippincraft. What do you make of it?
HIPPINCRAFT (Hugh Paddick)	Well, I'm afraid you're all wrong and I personally find it rather unpleasant. It's old, it's a rather startling blue — the lines are crude, functional and it was obviously thrown together in a hurry — to sati[?] the popular taste of the period. Very nasty. Yech!
Douglas Smith	Full marks, Hippincraft. It is, in fact, this week's script of Round T[?] Horne.
ORCHESTRA	**SIGNATURE TUNE**
Kenneth Horne	Hello and welcome to the show. I'd like to start off with an apology. you are probably aware, all the characters who appear in the show a[?] fictitious — particularly Kenneth Williams ...
Kenneth Williams	It's a disgrace.
Kenneth Horne	... and therefore, stranger than truth. These characters — in order no[?] give offence — (*laughs to himself*) are clothed in what we hope are fictitious names. But sometimes nature imitates art and therefore I wo[?] like to take this opportunity to apologise to the Very Reverend Ignati[?] Niblung-Goosecreature for the use of his name in a recent script. No[?] similarity was intended, and as a token of goodwill I trust that the Reverend gentleman will accept this voucher for six water skiing less[?] and a flask of Laidlaws Bland Goat Purge — in which to drink our health. Bottoms up Reverend Goosecreature. Smith —
Douglas Smith	Sir?
Kenneth Horne	Announce the next item.
ORCHESTRA	**ARMPIT THEATRE MUSIC**
Douglas Smith	And now — Armpit Theatre presents the story of a humble butler and[?] unswerving devotion to duty as he butles with the elements. Here ther[?] 'The Admirable Loombucket'.
ORCHESTRA	**MUSIC**
LORD HORSEPOSTURE (Kenneth Horne)	My name is Lord Tantamount Horseposture. I have my quarterings on[?] scutcheon — but that's another story. There have always been

Horsepostures in Berkshire, but that too is another story, not unconnected with the first one. Our story begins in the year 1912. I was giving a small dinner party at my country seat, Horseposture Hoo — to celebrate the engagement of my daughter, Wisteria, to the Reverend Isambard Mousepractice. As was usual on these occasions, my butler, the suave, impeccable Loombucket, was announcing the guests.

LOOMBUCKET (Kenneth Williams)	Lord Grisley Makeshift and his niece — he says — Mrs Costello Funf. Lady Jocasta Primp. Lady! Huh! The Right Horrible Narcissus Lestrange and friend. We've all got their number, ducky.
LORD HORSEPOSTURE	Loombucket — just announce them — we don't want a running commentary.
LOOMBUCKET	Very good, my Lord. Raving Jim Grunt and the Pubes. The Panderbody Sisters and Armitage the musical seal. The Luton Girls Choir. The Massed Bands of the Brigade of Guards. The Millwall Supporters Club. Officers and men of the United States Sixth Fleet. Bertram Mills Circus.
F/X	**CROWD NOISES BUILDING DURING THE ABOVE**
LORD HORSEPOSTURE	I have a feeling we sent out too many invitations. Loombucket.
LOOMBUCKET	Yes my lord?
LORD HORSEPOSTURE	I think you'd better send out for another half bottle of gin.
LOOMBUCKET	I already have, my lord — *and* a packet of cheese and onion flavoured crisps.
LORD HORSEPOSTURE	Loombucket, you think of everything.
LOOMBUCKET	I do no more than my duty sir.
LORD HORSEPOSTURE	I'm surprised that a man of your ability should be content to remain a humble butler.
LOOMBUCKET	I know my station, my lord. Piccadilly on Saturday night, If you hang about by the ticket machine you're sure to click for a gash bird. Besides sir, you and me — we're different. You have something that I haven't. It's called . . .
LORD HORSEPOSTURE	Breeding, Loombucket?
LOOMBUCKET	No sir. The second housemaid. The one with the frizzy hair and the enormous . . .
LORD HORSEPOSTURE	Loombucket!
LOOMBUCKET	I couldn't have put it better myself sir. I must attend to your guests. There's a Millwall supporter over there without a beer bottle to throw.
LORD HORSEPOSTURE	Oh and try and keep the Sixth Fleet away from the Luton Girls Choir. Introduce them to the elephants.
LOOMBUCKET	Very good sir. Ah, here comes your daughter — the lovely Wisteria.
LORD HORSEPOSTURE	She looks radiant tonight.
LOOMBUCKET	Indeed she does my lord. May I voice an opinion?
LORD HORSEPOSTURE	Yes Loombucket.

LOOMBUCKET	Well sir, with due propriety — I'd like to get her in the broom cupboa and . . .
LORD HORSEPOSTURE	Yes — Loombucket — attend to your duties.
WISTERIA (Betty Marsden)	(approaching, young — naïve) Oh, daddy, daddy, it's a lovely party. Isambard and I are having a lovely time.
ISAMBARD (Hugh Paddick)	We can't thank you enough Lord Horseposture. I hope I can make yo daughter happy.
WISTERIA	So do I Isambard.
LORD HORSEPOSTURE	Take care of her my boy. She's all I've got. At least she's all I've got t I'm giving you.
WISTERIA	Daddy, look what Loombucket gave me.
LORD HORSEPOSTURE	Good heavens. I thought you could only get those in Tokyo. You know, Isambard, old Loombucket's got quite a soft spot for Wisteria.
WISTERIA	Yes, daddy. He told me. It's his mattress.
ISAMBARD	How dare he. He's a servant. I mean — we're in different classes. The world is divided into us and them. We're us — and he's one of them.
LORD HORSEPOSTURE	Don't get upset on your engagement night. Here, I've got a present fo you Isambard. It belonged to my grandfather.
WISTERIA	Oh daddy, it's beautiful. See how the light reflects its myriad colours.
ISAMBARD	Is it the Koh-i-noor?
LORD HORSEPOSTURE	No. It's a boiled sweet.
ISAMBARD	But sir, it's yours. I don't want to take it.
LORD HORSEPOSTURE	No, do have it. If you suck it long enough it changes to green.
WISTERIA	Thank you daddy — thank you — thank you — thank you.
LORD HORSEPOSTURE	There's more to come.
ISAMBARD	Not a peppermint?
LORD HORSEPOSTURE	No. Even better. I'm going to take you on a cruise round the world —
WISTERIA	A cruise.
ISAMBARD	Round the world.
LORD HORSEPOSTURE	On my private yacht. (calls) Loombucket.
LOOMBUCKET	Sir?
LORD HORSEPOSTURE	We're going on a cruise — we'll be away for a whole year.
LOOMBUCKET	Very good sir. I take it you'll be requiring a packed lunch.
WISTERIA	You're coming too, Loombucket.
LOOMBUCKET	Round the world? To see far off places — to visit native bazaars and exot temples — to bathe in sun-kissed seas and toast my nubile limbs on fa distant sands — 'neath the blessed shade of sheltering palms — days o

	gay adventures and nights of tropic romance. Is that what you have in mind?
LORD HORSEPOSTURE	That's it exactly. Well, are you coming?
LOOMBUCKET	Oh alright. But it won't be the same as Mrs Brownjohn's at Skegness.
ORCHESTRA	**SEA MUSIC**
F/X	**SHIP'S ENGINES, STORM BLOWING UP**
Douglas Smith	Four months later found Lord Horseposture's two-thousand ton luxury craft the S.S. Saucy Mrs Trussport, ploughing across the South Pacific
CAPTAIN RUMSPIGOT (Bill Pertwee)	Excuse me, Lord Horseposture.
LORD HORSEPOSTURE	What is it Captain Rumspigot?
CAPTAIN RUMSPIGOT	There's a force eight blowing up sir. I don't know if the old tub can take it
LORD HORSEPOSTURE	Well can you Mrs Rumspigot?
MRS RUMPSPIGOT (Betty Marsden)	Aye aye dearie. I can take it and dish it out.
CAPTAIN RUMSPIGOT	We're only making four knots sir. If we don't get our knots up we're done for.
LORD HORSEPOSTURE	I'll have a word with Loombucket. Ahoy there!
LOOMBUCKET	(*off mike*) Yes my lord?
LORD HORSEPOSTURE	Row a bit faster, there's a good chap.
LOOMBUCKET	I can't sir. I've caught a crab — and I'm dressing it for dinner.
LORD HORSEPOSTURE	Don't bother — we're dining informally tonight.
F/X	**ROLL OF THUNDER**
WISTERIA	Oh daddy — daddy — what's that?
LORD HORSEPOSTURE	It's a man behind that curtain waggling a sheet of zinc.
CAPTAIN RUMSPIGOT	Tis the sound that mariners dread most — next to time gentlemen please. Tis a typhoon.
F/X	**WIND HOWLING**
WISTERIA	Oh hold me Isambard.
CAPTAIN RUMSPIGOT	Hold your own Isambard miss. I've got me hands full.
ISAMBARD	Don't worry darling. I'm here with you.
CAPTAIN RUMSPIGOT	Thankee sweetheart. You'm be a comfort to an old sailor.
F/X	**SPLINTERING CRASH**
LORD HORSEPOSTURE	She's breaking up. We're sinking. Man the lifeboats.
CAPTAIN RUMSPIGOT	They've been swept away.
LORD HORSEPOSTURE	What have we got that floats?

LOOMBUCKET	I had the foresight to bring along this self-inflatable rubber Douglas Smith —
Douglas Smith	(*as life raft — hisses*)
LORD HORSEPOSTURE	Well done, Smith.
Douglas Smith	Thank you sir. (*as life raft — hisses*) Pft — pft — pft.
LORD HORSEPOSTURE	Alright Smith. What is it?
Douglas Smith	I think I've got a slow puncture.
LORD HORSEPOSTURE	Don't build your part Smith. You're perfectly watertight and you know it.
Douglas Smith	I thought I'd work in a bit of pathos.
LOOMBUCKET	Shut up. Right, man the Douglas Smith — women and children first.
ORCHESTRA	**MUSIC LINK**
LORD HORSEPOSTURE	For days we bobbed up and down, the waves lapping round our Douglas Smith. No land to be seen anywhere — the hot sun beating down — but thanks to Loombucket, we were still alive.
F/X	**WAVES LAPPING**
LOOMBUCKET	Please sir — it's been eight days now — may I come aboard? It's pretty tiring swimming along pulling you.
ISAMBARD	Oh good gracious me — we can't share our quarters with the servants.
WISTERIA	It's terribly presumptuous of you Loombucket.
LOOMBUCKET	I wouldn't ask but for the last four days I've had this shark gnawing at my leg.
LORD HORSEPOSTURE	Alright. Come aboard if you must, but don't bring that shark with you. There's barely enough food for the rest of us.
WISTERIA	Oh don't be so mean daddy, the shark won't eat much — just Loombucket — and we can spare him.
LOOMBUCKET	Thank you me lady.
LORD HORSEPOSTURE	Any ideas where we are Loombucket?
LOOMBUCKET	Bottom of page twenty-three sir.
LORD HORSEPOSTURE	Good. For a moment I thought we were lost.
WISTERIA	Daddy, look, a sailing ship.
CAPTAIN RUMSPIGOT	Give her a hail.
LORD HORSEPOSTURE	Ahoy there —
CAPTAIN AHAB (Hugh Paddick)	(*off mike*) Ahoy there — who be you?
LORD HORSEPOSTURE	I be Lord Horseposture — this week. Who be you?
CAPTAIN AHAB	I be Captain Ahab — I be looking for Moby Dick. For twenty years I've sailed the seas looking for that accursed Leviathan. D'you see this wooden leg matey? I got this from Moby Dick.

Kenneth Williams	(*snide*) I bet it looked better on him than it does on you.
CAPTAIN AHAB	They say I'm mad because I've sworn to revenge myself on him — are you sure you haven't seen a great white whale pass this way?
LORD HORSEPOSTURE	We've got some anchovies you can have.
CAPTAIN AHAB	Tis no use. I'm condemned to sail the Atlantic Ocean till I find him.
CAPTAIN RUMSPIGOT	But this be the South Pacific. What are you doing here?
CAPTAIN AHAB	I don't know. I don't write this rubbish. Goodbye.
WISTERIA	Can't you pick us up?
CAPTAIN AHAB	Sorry I can't. I'm in a different plot. Farewell.
WISTERIA	He's gone sob sob gulp gasp. It's no use. We could just drift on like this for ever (*herself*) just because the writers can't think of a tag. I can't stand any more. I can't stand it.
Hugh Paddick	There there. Steady on, Betty old girl. She's right you know. It's not fair on her, poor old duck, dragging her out these cold mornings — I mean she's lost a morning's work — five shillings an hour she gets for cleaning, don't you Bett?
Betty Marsden	Yes — and me lunch thrown in.
Kenneth Williams	Take no notice, she's just trying to get a bit of cheap sympathy. What about me — look what I have to put up with. I've never been properly serviced in this show —not once.
Bill Pertwee	What about me. I have to come all the way from Hove on the early train, and I have to tie string round me trousers — and smoke a clay pipe before they'll let me on the cheap workman's.
Hugh Paddick	Well I've had enough. We none of us get serviced except him — Lord Muck Horne.
OMNES	AD LIB — AGGRESSIVE MUMBLING
Kenneth Horne	Back — back you mutinous dogs. You see what I've got in my hand.
OMNES	SHARP INTAKE OF BREATH
Kenneth Horne	Yes. It's a script of the Clitheroe Kid and I'm not afraid to read it.
Kenneth Williams	You wouldn't dare.
Kenneth Horne	Oh wouldn't I? Page one. Sound effect of door opening. Hello Mother — Hello Grandpa. Hello Jimmy. Goodbye Mother. Goodbye Grandpa. Goodbye Jimmy. Sound effect of door closing.
Kenneth Williams	Alright, we've had enough. We know when we're beaten. Alright, back to the plot.
Kenneth Horne	And in future — watch it. Come on, Smith.
Douglas Smith	Could you do a bit more of the Clitheroe Kid. I was quite enjoying it. It's a jolly sight funnier than the stuff *we* get.
Kenneth Horne	Alright Smith. I'll read you some more at bedtime.
Douglas Smith	And Winnie the Pooh?

Kenneth Horne	Yes, if you're good.
Douglas Smith	Thanks. (*clears throat*) Twenty-five days they drifted and then at last . . . .
ISAMBARD (Hugh Paddick)	Land . . . .
F/X	**LONG DRAWN OUT SHIP HITTING ROCK**
ISAMBARD	Ho!
ORCHESTRA	**PLAY OFF**
Kenneth Horne	Where had we landed? What was to become of us? How do we get away with it? Assuming that nobody answers the third question correctly we'll be back next week with part two of The Admirable Loombucket.
	(*The second episode described their adventures on a South Sea island. Eventually Loombucket was thrown into a volcano, played by Douglas Smith with lava running down his sides. A fitting end!*)
Kenneth Horne	But now it's time for the Admirable Fraser Hayes Four who have received a special dispensation of Doctor Cattermole's lightning rejuvenator — which has enabled them to get here to sing.
...ASER HAYES FOUR ...RCHESTRA	**MUSIC BREAK**
	(*applause*)
Douglas Smith	And now the Round The Horne Colour Supplement.
Kenneth Horne	First in the kitchen — but last in the bathroom — our cookery expert, Daphne Whitethigh, with another of her classic recipes.

DAPHNE WHITETHIGH (Betty Marsden)	This week I'm going to tell you some of the many interesting things you can do with a yak. There's yak à l'orange, yak pasties, yak kebab, yak fingers, yak on a spit — and yak in its jacket. But my family's favourite is a simply scrumptious dessert — coupe yak. Take your yak, pluck it and bone it — take an ordinary saucepan, the type you use for broiling hippopotamus, when it's tender, cool it and smother it in raspberry ice cream, sprinkle on a little ground coconut — three tons should be enough — and serve with a hip bath of custard. Some people claim that the coconut and raspberry ice cream disguise the natural flavour of the yak meat — but when I served *my* husband with it his immediate reaction on tasting it was —

107

MR WHITETHIGH (Hugh Paddick)	Yak!
DAPHNE WHITETHIGH	Next week I shall be telling you how to make Mongoose flavoured yoghourt.
Kenneth Horne	I shall be interested to hear how she gets the lumps out. Now — on the London Beat, Sunday night personality, Seamus Android.
SEAMUS ANDROID (Bill Pertwee)	Well now — alright — hallo. Well we've had our little bit of fun — and before we get on — I've had a number of requests from viewers asking me if I would — but unfortunately I can't — alright. Now standing beside me I have a man who has not only been — but come back, and has written a book about it. Now sir, I'd like to ask you one last question before we begin — how does it feel to? Because although I have, I know many of our listeners haven't themselves personally although I have . . . myself personally. In person myself. And with that I return you to the studio.
Kenneth Horne	Thank you Seamus Android. Every Sunday night when I watch your show — I'm speechless — and that makes two of us. Now with a quick round-up of with-it happenings in London this week — Brad Smallpiece.
BRAD SMALLPIECE (Hugh Paddick)	Well there's Massed Goat Pandering at the Royal Nobblers Institute. Knock a Rabbi out of bed at Battersea fun fair in aid of the Stuffed Mouse for Thailand fund. Hip Throbbing at Whipsnade, Finger Bogling at the Spotted Dick Memorial Hall, Hammersmith and an exhibition of Gnome Clenching in the corset department of Sparkslew and Towser, chiropodists by appointment to ex-queen Marie of Rumania — Clapham. But I myself will make a beeline for the Master Carpenters Knot Hole Of The Year contest which will be held in the saloon bar of the Orang-Utan's Arms, Stoke Poges.
Kenneth Horne	You'll be able to see it at home via the Early Bird Satellite. This week the Colour Supplement turns its attention to The Englishman's Home. According to song writers there are many sorts of home. You can have a little grey one in the West — a house is not one, and it's the place you hang your hat. But if that's to be believed I've been living in a broom closet for years. And what — again according to song writers — do people want from a home. Well, they demand somewhere where buffalo roam and deer and antelope play. It's alright if you've got a daily woman but most inconvenient if you live in a bed sitter. Believe me I've tried it and I know. They upset the baboons — and then there was that unfortunate misunderstanding between a buffalo and my wife's fur coat. There were a few discouraging words heard *that* day. Sill I won't dwell on it. I expect you've got troubles of your own. Now the joys of home ownership aren't all they're cracked up to be — particularly if you've got noisy neighbours.
Betty Marsden	(*cockney*) Jim!
Bill Pertwee	(*cockney*) Hello.
Betty Marsden	(*cockney*) They're at it again next door, Jim. I can't stand living here next to them — well I mean foreigners coming in and out at all times of the day and night — the police outside the door and parties every night of the week — and they never invite us in. I can't stand them people next door Jim. We've got to move.
Bill Pertwee	(*cockney*) We can't dear. Not as long as I'm Chancellor of the Exchequer.
ORCHESTRA	**BRIEF MUSIC LINK**

Kenneth Horne	Of course, not everybody has a home and not everybody wants one. There have been many songs extolling the virtues of the vagrant life, and who more fitting to sing one than Rambling Syd Rumpo.
RAMBLING SYD (Kenneth Williams)	Hello me deario — for I'll nadger my greebles on the open road — and rumble my gander can — till all the seas run dry or until I get spots before my eyes — whichever comes first.
Kenneth Horne	I think it's six to four on spots before the eyes. Well, Syd, I believe you're going to sing us a song of the open road.
RAMBLING SYD	I am. Tis a song I composed myself and is autobiographical in parts. It tells of the carefree life led by the hobo — or as he's known in America, the lower spine. There are one or two words I ought to explain before I burst forth with my air — for instance, take 'wogglers' —
Kenneth Horne	No thanks. They don't agree with me.
RAMBLING SYD	They are old English for a part of the rabbit, and are considered a delicacy by we gentlemen of the road. It's roughly the bit that keeps the pie crust up. You may scoff at such mean fare but if you stew a rabbit's wogglers in an old tin can over an open fire, you can't conceive what disgusting muck it is. And so to my song — which tells of the joys of the free gypsy life.

GUITAR ACCOMPANIMENT

Oh what care I for a goose feather cot,
Plumpo — plumpo.
What care I for a grunge in the pot,
A fine fat grummit all piping hot,
I'm content with what I've got,
For I am old Syd Rumpo.

What do I need with dumplings fine,
Dumpo — dumpo.
I'm content with a jug of wine,
A brace of moulies will suit me fine,
On rabbit's wogglers will I dine —
For I am old Syd Rumpo.

What need I for scrumptious wife,
Scrumpo — scrumpo.
Oh I'm content with the gypsy life,
My only friend my traddling knife,
For wedlock only leads to strife —
And one day a little Rumpo.

(*applause*)

Kenneth Horne	Thank you Rambling Syd. May your pot never be grungeless. Sometimes I swear I understand every word I say. But whatever the joys of a vagrant life, most of us want a place of our own.
TAPE	**'ROOM WITH A VIEW'**
BINKIE HUCKABACK (Hugh Paddick)	Happy darling?
CELIA MOLESTRANGLER (Betty Marsden)	I'd be happy anywhere with you Charles.

BINKIE	Oh Fiona — I know it's not what you're used to — it's terribly cramped and poky, but it's ours.
CELIA	It's home Charles.
BINKIE	And don't spare the horses? Ha ha.
CELIA	Oh Charles, I love you when you're brittle.
BINKIE	I'd do anything to make you happy darling. Oh I know it may be hell for you living here — but it won't be for long.
CELIA	I don't care how long it is — as long as I'm with you. But I don't mind living here Charles. It's pleasant — there are plenty of windows. It's a nice view.
BINKIE	Yes, we're lucky really Fiona. The hustle and bustle of Piccadilly outside our window. We were lucky to get this place.
CELIA	Living here — we're never lonely — always people popping in. I don't mind during the day — it's company for me, but at night Charles — there are no curtains at the windows and the light's always on.
BINKIE	Yes, it's not easy for us — but what can you do when you're living in a telephone box. Kiss me Fiona.
CELIA	Oh Charles. (*kiss*)
F/X	**BUTTON 'B' BEING PRESSED AND PENNIES DROPPING INTO CUP**
BINKIE	Oh. We've hit the jackpot.

ORCHESTRA	**BRIEF LINK**
Kenneth Horne	For a lot of people home is not just where you live, but a place to entertain your friends. At least that's what I think, and recently when I celebrated my birthday I decided to throw a party. Well I didn't want the trouble of catering myself, so when I saw an advert in one of the glossies which said 'Bona Caterers — We Can Handle Everything' I gave them a ring and next morning —
F/X	**DOOR CHIMES**
F/X	**DOOR OPENS**
Kenneth Horne	Good morning.
JULIAN (Hugh Paddick)	Hello — I'm Julian and this is my friend, Sandy.
SANDY (Kenneth Williams)	We are your Bona Caterers — that is to say — Jule and me — we can cater for every function.
JULIAN	From your Hunt Ball down to your intimate at 'ome.
SANDY	Just give us a free hand and we'll give you a do your guests will never forget.
JULIAN	Now what's the occasion?
Kenneth Horne	It's my birthday party. I'm thirty-nine.
JULIAN	D'you hear that Sand — thirty-nine.
SANDY	Round the neck he's thirty-nine. Hm — so you'll want a cake.
JULIAN	We can do you something pretty bizarre in marzipan.
SANDY	How about Dundee, Jule?
JULIAN	Yes — I could let myself go in Dundee.
SANDY	He could let himself go in Dundee Mr Horne — he could.
JULIAN	Or I could do something provocative in a sponge — with a fruit filling.
SANDY	Yes in three tiers — with a motif.
Kenneth Horne	What sort of motif?
SANDY	Well, the sort of thing people are associated with. For Ringo Starr we done a set of drums — for Stirling Moss we done a racing car and for Sandie Shaw we done a huge pair of feet in marzipan.
JULIAN	With glacé cherries for toenails.
Kenneth Horne	I think just a simple cake — and what about the rest of the food?
JULIAN	It depends on what sort you have in mind. I mean you can have your standing up running or your sit down knife and fork.
SANDY	Your stand up fingers works out cheaper.
Kenneth Horne	Yes, I think a cold buffet is best.
SANDY	Would you like us to lay on a turkey?

Kenneth Horne	Well I hadn't planned on a cabaret.
SANDY	Oh he's bold!
JULIAN	He goes too far. Now drinkettes. What do you plan there treash?
SANDY	Well two dozen bottles of Egg Nog for a start.
Kenneth Horne	But I don't know anybody that drinks Egg Nog.
JULIAN	We do, Heartface.
SANDY	He likes his Egg Nog, Jule does. Three Egg Nogs and he lets his riah right down — don't you Jule?
JULIAN	Yes. Gin makes me maudlin.
SANDY	And you don't want him maudlin all over your guests. He gets quite lachrymose on the gin and he blurts it all out — about Bognor. He had an experience in Bognor didn't you Jule.
JULIAN	Yes. Very naff it was, and when I've been on the gin it all wells up in me.
SANDY	And up comes Bognor.
JULIAN	And we don't want Bognor coming up.
SANDY	So it's two dozen bottles of Egg Nog.
Kenneth Horne	I didn't know you were coming.
JULIAN	Course we're coming. We wouldn't miss a party that Mick Jagger was at.
Kenneth Horne	Mick Jagger — I haven't invited him.

JULIAN	We have — and David Frost and Peter Cook and Dudley Moore.
SANDY	You've got to have your actual celebs, or you'll never get reported in the glossies.
JULIAN	You want to see your eek in the glossies.
Kenneth Horne	And what about my other guests.
SANDY	Well let's have a look at your list. Hmm. Don't want him. He sounds dull. She must be eighty if she's a day. No they're out — they're all out.
Kenneth Horne	But that only leaves me.
SANDY	Sorry ducky but you're out as well. With the people we've invited you just wouldn't fit in.
ORCHESTRA	**PAY OFF**
Kenneth Horne	Of course I argued with them and in the end they relented and let me come Not as a guest, of course — I was in charge of the cloakroom — made thirty shillings in tips — so it wasn't a dead loss.
	Well, that's the end of our show except for a police message — to all motorists in the English Channel — you should have turned left at Dover. Cheerio — see you next week.
	(*applause*)
ORCHESTRA	**'ROUND THE HORNE' PLAYOUT**

114

ROUND THE HORNE

3RD SERIES — PROGRAMME NO. 11
TRANSMISSION: Sunday 23rd April 1967:
1.30-2.00 p.m. LIGHT PROGRAMME

Douglas Smith	Hello — this is Douglas — 'I dreamt I went to the Opera dressed only in my Dobbitex Medical Cummerbund' — Smith. For the next half-hour we invite you to turn down the lights, roll back the carpet, strip down the walls, fill in the cracks, upholster the settee, shampoo the dog, put out the cat, wax polish your grannie — in fact do anything rather than listen t 'Round The Horne'.
ORCHESTRA	**SIGNATURE TUNE**
Kenneth Horne	Hello. That was Douglas Smith who would like to clear something up - and so he should — he spilled it. Now, today, as everyone knows, is Festoon A Gnome With Bacon Rind Day, and to mark the occasion, London is in festive mood. At Aldgate there's an exhibition of Chicken Trembling given by the Ladbroke Grov Buddhist Girl Pipers. At Chiswick Baths there's the washroom attendants' annual flannel dance and zabaglione show. There's Barrister Nudging a Kew and the two man inter-Rabbi bob sled championships will be held as usual down the escalators at Leicester Square tube station — weather an platform tickets permitting. But I myself will head for the Muffin Monger Hall, Cheapside, where the over eighties Nudist Glee Club are holding their Bring and Buy Sale. I'm interested in, not so much *what* they bring a what they bring it *in*. Smith — make the announcement.
Douglas Smith	And now Armpit Theatre presents a story of the heyday of the Edwardia Music Hall — The Phantom of Bogmouth Hip.
ORCHESTRA	**MUSIC (EDWARDIAN PIT BAND)**
THROBWALLOPER (Kenneth Horne)	My name is C. B. Throbwalloper. I am a theatrical impressario. My theat was the Bogmouth Hippodrome. But what, in 1910, was a thriving Musi Hall is now a Supermarket. It's sad really to think that in the spot where Little Tich once danced there's now twopence off liver sausage, and that i Harry Lauder were alive, he'd be singing 'A wee doch and doris' on the bacon slicer. But in 1910 Variety was booming and every evening I would go backstage and stand in the wings encouraging the chorus girls befor they went on . . . . Good evening Gladys.
GLADYS (Betty Marsden)	Good (*squeal*) Mr Throbwalloper.
THROBWALLOPER	Good evening Marjorie.
MARJORIE (Betty Marsden)	Good (*squeal*) Mr Throbwalloper.
THROBWALLOPER	Good evening Bubbles.
OAKROYD (Bill Pertwee)	Good — Oi! Watch it mate.
THROBWALLOPER	Sorry Mr Oakroyd, it's terribly dark back here. How's the show going?
OAKROYD	Very well Mr Throbwalloper. The Amazing Grotty and his educated Alsatian Baldwin are on now — listen.
Kenneth Williams	(*sings*) Tell me, tell me where do you roam, shipmates of mine.
F/X	**DISTANT SMATTERING OF APPLAUSE**
THROBWALLOPER	He's not very good is he.

OAKROYD	No sir — but it's not bad for a dog. Look he's going to do his trick now.
AMAZING GROTTY (Hugh Paddick)	And now Ladies and Gentlemen, Baldwin the almost human canine will give you a little demonstration of — stop it Baldwin — of canine acumen and calculating — stop it Baldwin, bad dog. I hold up my — Baldwin — down sir — my hand, and Baldwin will — naughty dog. Baldwin will tell me the number of fingers I'm holding up. Are you ready Baldwin?
BALDWIN (Kenneth Williams)	(barks once)
AMAZING GROTTY	Now how many fingers am I holding up?
BALDWIN	(barks three times)
AMAZING GROTTY	Wrong. I'm holding up four.
BALDWIN	(snarls and snaps)
AMAZING GROTTY	(yelps) Quite right Baldwin, it is three . . . now. And now, ladies and gentlemen, Baldwin will show you his novel way of riding this one-wheel cycle. Stop it Baldwin — bad dog. Come back.
ORCHESTRA	**PIT BAND TYPE PLAYOFF**
F/X	**ENORMOUS CROWD BOOING, HISSING AND CAT CALLING**
THROBWALLOPER	Who's next?
OAKROYD	Sid and Elsie Huxtable —
THROBWALLOPER	Ah yes. In Neddie the pantomime horse. That always goes well. The kiddies love it.
ORCHESTRA	**FIRST FEW BARS 'IN THE SHADOWS' (PIT BAND STYLE)**
F/X	**ENORMOUS EXPLOSION**
THROBWALLOPER	Good heavens. Neddie has exploded — the entire back has been ripped off. Quick — bring down the curtain.
ORCHESTRA	**PUNCTUATING DRAMATIC CHORD**
THROBWALLOPER	We all rushed to the horse and unzipped the skin — but it was too late. Sid Huxtable had perished — miraculously Elsie, although suffering from shock and slightly charred — was in one piece.
OAKROYD	What happened Miss Elsie?
ELSIE (Betty Marsden)	I don't know. One minute we was trotting round doing our equestrian gavotte with Sid in the back as usual reading the paper, then he lit his pipe and — suddenly bang! He was heading for the last round up.
THROBWALLOPER	Via the roof.
ELSIE	I can't understand it. He's never gone off like this before.
THROBWALLOPER	Lit his pipe you say. (sniffs) That's odd. Oakroyd?
OAKROYD	Yes sir?

THROBWALLOPER	Put your head in that skin — what do you make of it?
OAKROYD	It smells like a mixture of Old Hobson's Curly Cut and gas.
THROBWALLOPER	Precisely. Gas. Somebody filled the skin with gas. Didn't you realise Mrs Huxtable?
ELSIE	Up the front end you don't know what's going on. Besides I get plenty of fre[sh] air through the nostrils — who could have done this terrible thing?
THROBWALLOPER	I don't know. I'll have a word with lovable old Pop the stage door keeper — see if he noticed anything unusual this evening. (*calls*) Pop.
POP (Kenneth Williams)	Yes Mr Throbwalloper?
THROBWALLOPER	Sid Huxtable has gone, Pop.
POP	Yes I heard him. That's the seventieth fatal accident this week, and it's only Tuesday.
THROBWALLOPER	Something tells me it's more than a coincidence lovable old Pop. It looks lik[e] the work of a maniac.
POP	What does?
THROBWALLOPER	This script — However — Look at the way they've died. First house Monday we discovered that Nosmo the india rubber man had perished — We found him stretched out from here to Walthamstow. Second house, the death defying McWhirters failed to live up to their bill matter, and Tiny Tim Gruber the mannikin of mirth — was found impaled on a paper clip. And now poor Sid Huxtable's gone. Who could have done such a terrible thing?
POP	Who could have done it? You may well ask. Old Pop knows a thing or two — old Pop knows more than he's saying — It's no good you asking old Pop cos old Pop ain't telling. There's no flies on old Pop — old Pop will carry the secret to his grave, old Pop will. (*exits laughing insanely*)
F/X	**FOOTSTEPS AWAY**
	(*pause*)
F/X	**FOOTSTEPS RETURN**
POP	(*returns laughing insanely*) P.S. I done it. I killed them all — I admit it, [I] confess. I killed Nosmo *and* the flying McWhirters *and* Tiny Tim Gruber *and* I blew up Sid Huxtable, and I'm glad I tell you, glad. And they won't be the last. I'll kill you all — Ha ha ha ha etc. (*exits laughing*)
THROBWALLOPER	I think he knows more than he's saying.
ORCHESTRA	**PUNCTUATING CHORD**
OAKROYD	As the week progressed we awaited each day with trepidation. Every performance brought a new disaster. On Wednesday it was Enrico Nurds the Basso profundo.
ENRICO NURDS (Kenneth Horne)	(*sings*) Down among the dead men let me . . .
F/X	**GUNSHOT**
ENRICO NURDS	(*sings*) . . . lie.

120

F/X	**FALLING BODY**
OAKROYD	On Thursday — Kardinski the prestidigitator.
ORCHESTRA	**(SOFTLY IN BACKGROUND) 'AFTER THE BALL'**
KARDINSKI (Hugh Paddick)	As you see, this paper bag is completely empty and yet from thin air I produce the jack of hearts, the ten of spades, the queen of diamonds, a live hand grenade, the two of clubs, the three of . . . a live hand grenade?? Now I wonder where . . .
F/X	**EXPLOSION**
OAKROYD	On Friday it was Fazackerly and Pubes, cross talk comedians.
FAZACKERLY (Hugh Paddick)	Ladies and gentlemen a little recitation entitled 'Dick Turpin's Ride to York'. Twas on a dark and stormy night when Dick his Bess did mount, when . . .
PUBES (Kenneth Williams)	'Ere. Do you like conundrums.
FAZACKERLY	Yes, I like conundrums.
PUBES	Well then. What is it that's long, black and shiny with poisonous fangs?
FAZACKERLY	I don't know. What *is* it that's long, black and shiny with poisonous fangs?
PUBES	It's a black Mamba.
FAZACKERLY	A black Mamba? I don't get it.
PUBES	Well you soon will. One's just crawled up your trouser leg.
FAZACKERLY	I don't wish to know that. Ladies and gentlemen, a little monologue entitled 'Dick Turk Turpin's Ride to (*screams*) Yawk!'
OAKROYD	On Saturday it was the turn of Sunny Goatpractice V.A.F. the lady ventriloquist extraordinaire.
SUNNY (Betty Marsden)	Now tell me Johnny — what did you learn at school today? (*as dummy*) I learned to say my alphabet. (*Sunny*) You learned to say your alphabet? (*dummy*) Yes. (*Sunny*) Would you like to say it now? (*dummy*) Yes. (*Sunny*) Very good, and while little Johnny is saying his alphabet I will smoke this cigarette and drink this glass of (*smacks lips*) Prussic acid . . . (*dummy*) Glimey, I've geen koisened!
F/X	**BODY HITTING FLOOR**
THROBWALLOPER	That night after the curtain came down I stayed behind in the empty theatre engaged in the usual duties of a busy theatre manager — falsifying the returns, embezzling the petty cash and stealing the soap. Perhaps I would find some clue to the mysterious events of the past week in the theatre archives. I sat there leafing through some faded yellowing chorus girls — when I heard a noise backstage. I decided to investigate. I crept stealthily onto the darkened stage.
F/X	**FOOTSTEPS ON CREAKING FLOOR BOARDS**
THROBSWALLOPER	Hello is there anybody there?
JULIAN (Hugh Paddick)	Oh hello — I'm Julian and this is my friend Sandy.

THROBWALLOPER	Not yet. You're not on till the second half.
SANDY (Kenneth Williams)	Oh — sorry we spoke. Come on Jule, back to the pub.
ORCHESTRA	**SINISTER MUSIC**
THROBWALLOPER	What was that?
Edwin Braden	It was us Ken.
Kenneth Horne	Oh, it was you Braden. Thank heavens. For a moment I thought it was the maniac. Come to think of it I'd feel safer if it was.
POP	*(off mike) (cackles madly)*
THROBWALLOPER	Suddenly I saw him — Pop. So it was you Pop.
POP	Don't Pop me —
THROBWALLOPER	I hadn't intended to. You'll have to do it yourself. But you've killed over eighty people. Why? Why? You're mad.
POP	Far from mad Mr Throbwalloper. Far from it. Well not that far. I commute.
THROBWALLOPER	What was your motive for committing these crimes?
POP	I have worked it all out. You see I am in line for the throne.
THROBWALLOPER	You?
POP	Yes. There are only twenty-three million eight hundred and forty-six thousand nine hundred and four people standing between me and the throne of England. When I've killed them all I shall be the Queen. And then . . . ha ha . . . and then . . . when I am the Queen I shall be able to get in up the Cup Final for nothing.
THROBWALLOPER	You fiend. You won't get away with it.
POP	Oh won't I.
F/X	**RUNNING FOOTSTEPS**
THROBWALLOPER	I chased him across the stage and into the auditorium — He tried to elude me but eventually I nabbed him in the stalls. We grappled. The fight was on. Take that — Thump.
POP	Grunt. Take that. Splat.
THROBWALLOPER	Groan. Take that. Kerpow.
POP	Grunt. Whimper.
THROBWALLOPER	Boing.
POP	Groan.
THROBWALLOPER	Whap.
POP	Pow!
THROBWALLOPER	Ping!

POP	Ping?
THROBWALLOPER	My braces have snapped.
POP	Oh — well I know when I'm beaten. I give up.
THROBWALLOPER	Take him away.
POP	You can't do this to me. I'm an insipient Queen. No no no (*exiting*).
ORCHESTRA	**PAY OFF CHORD**
Kenneth Horne	The poor quivering wreck was led away to a place where he could do no harm. A home for distressed Gentlefolk — or as it is better known, the BBC Television Centre. He was set to work on simple tasks that his poor fuddled mind could grasp — and he's now the producer of 'Till Death Us Do Part'. Well if it's not him it's someone very much like him. And so from one tragedy to another — Here are the Fraser Hayes Four — you may notice they sing a little flat. Well where they come from they're not allowed anything sharp. Ladies and Gentlemen, The Fraser Hayes Four.

FRASER HAYES FOUR **& ORCHESTRA**	**MUSIC BREAK**
	(*applause*)
Douglas Smith	And now the Round The Horne Colour Supplement.
Kenneth Horne	Women's Page. Here is Daphne Whitethigh to answer some of your personal queries.
DAPHNE WHITETHIGH (Betty Marsden)	First I'd like to answer a question that comes from Mrs J. P. of Aldershot. Now I realise that a mole on your hip is an unsightly thing, but don't worry. My opinion is that the mole is only hibernating and he'll go back to the garden when the fine weather comes. Next is a letter from Mrs Upjohn of Reigate — who complains that every night she's woken up by the screaming habdabs. What I would suggest is that the next time it happens you hammer on the wall and tell Mr and Mrs Habdab to shut up. Finally, I have a letter from Worried of Hampstead who wants to know how to acquire that fashionably wide-eyed look. The answer is simple. Wear very tight corsets.
Kenneth Horne	Thank you Daphne. I shall take your advice. Now once again it's time for our on the spot report from Sunday Night TV personality, Seamus Android.
SEAMUS ANDROID (Bill Pertwee)	Hello — Ha ha alright. Now then — er . . . ha ha — well that's enough of me. Well I know you're dying to meet my first guest so I'll just get on with boring you myself for the next two hours in person personally myself instead. Alright — Now — it's often been said and I would be the last to, as I *have* been, many times before and so there is nothing I can do. And with that — Goodnight.
Kenneth Horne	Thank you Seamus Android, a man of few words; the words being —
SEAMUS ANDROID	Well now — hello, alright.
Kenneth Horne	This week Round The Horne Colour Supplement takes a look at the Englishman and money. When you do have money — the first thing you should do is to insure yourself against losing it. Mind you, some policies are more useful than others. I myself have a policy which matures in the event of my being eaten alive by whelks on Shrove Tuesday. If this *does* happen, my wife receives a lump sum of seventeen and six and a glossy calendar depicting the man from the Pru riding his bike in the nude. Admittedly insurance companies take risks, and Lloyds of London will insure anything.
Hugh Paddick	Good morning sir.
OLD SCRUFFPOT (Kenneth Williams)	Good morning. I'd like to take out some insurance.
Hugh Paddick	Life?
OLD SCRUFFPOT	No. Me legs.
Hugh Paddick	Your legs?
OLD SCRUFFPOT	I want to insure them against theft or flood.
Hugh Paddick	Flood?

OLD SCRUFFPOT	Yes. I got a hole in my boot.
Hugh Paddick	How much were you thinking of insuring them for?
OLD SCRUFFPOT	I thought — a million pounds a leg. That's — let me see now — that's three million pounds. No *two*. I was counting my umbrella.
Hugh Paddick	Two million pounds? Isn't that rather excessive?
OLD SCRUFFPOT	Well Mistinguette insured her legs for a million — so mine must be worth double. I mean they're twice as thick for a start and much hairier. Besides I got valuable tattoos up me legs. I got the Hunt in full cry streaming up my left leg.
Hugh Paddick	Where's the fox? No — don't answer that. But what makes you think your legs are worth that kind of money?
OLD SCRUFFPOT	They are essential to my livelihood.
Hugh Paddick	Why? What do you do?
OLD SCRUFFPOT	I trip women up and run off with their handbags.
ORCHESTRA	**BRIEF LINK**

Kenneth Horne	Money plays an important part in every aspect of our lives — to the gambler it's easy come, easy go — but excessive gambling has ruined many marriages.
GRAM	'ROOM WITH A VIEW'
F/X	DOOR OPENING
DAME CELIA MOLESTRANGLER (Betty Marsden)	Charles is that you?
BINKIE HUCKABACK (Hugh Paddick)	Yes Fiona, it's me.
CELIA	Charles where have you been all night? I waited up but you didn't come home.
BINKIE	I've got a confession to make. It's gone — everything is lost.
CELIA	Everything?
BINKIE	Lost. Lost. Lost. They were playing for five hundred pounds a shoe.
CELIA	Chemmy Charles?
BINKIE	No. Strip Poker.
CELIA	But — is everything lost?
BINKIE	Lost. Yes, it's all gone on the turn of a card. My streak's run out. I can't complain.
CELIA	Everything? Has the house gone?
BINKIE	Yes, the house, the car, the business, and now you.
CELIA	What makes you think you've lost me?
BINKIE	Well he had a royal flush and I only had two pairs.
ORCHESTRA	BRIEF LINK
Kenneth Horne	The harder you work and the more money you earn — the more tax you have to pay. The only remedy is to get a good accountant and when I was recommended to a firm that specialised in handling the accounts of show business people, I went along straight away. The sign on the door said, Bona Tax Consultants.
F/X	DOOR OPENS
Kenneth Horne	Hello — anybody there?
JULIAN (Hugh Paddick)	Oh hello — I'm Julian and this is my friend Sandy.
SANDY (Kenneth Williams)	We're your actual accountants. He's chartered and I'm certified. What brings you trolling in here?
Kenneth Horne	I was recommended to you by a show business acquaintance of mine. To be precise the steam room attendant at the South Mimms Gents Slipper Baths a Go Go.

SANDY	Oh Gordon.
Kenneth Horne	He wishes to be remembered to you.
JULIAN	Gordon?
SANDY	Yes, you remember him — used to be in the Wardrobe at Elstree.
JULIAN	Oh *that* Gordon.
Kenneth Horne	Anyway he said you could help me with my tax returns.
SANDY	Hm yes. Well you'll have to let us have a vada at your assets.
Kenneth Horne	Do you have to?
SANDY	It's essential. But it's in the strictest confidence. We're like doctors aren't we Jule. We never divulge.
JULIAN	Never — we only ever use the information you give us in the preparation of your accounts and occasionally for a bit of blackmail.
Kenneth Horne	Well alright. Here are the details of my assets.
SANDY	Hmm! Oh you got one of them — two of them —
Kenneth Horne	Three actually. One's in my wife's name.
SANDY	We can't touch them — they're frozen.
JULIAN	We could huff on them.
SANDY	That's your gross turnover is it?
Kenneth Horne	Yes.
JULIAN	Very impressive. The tax man's going to be very hot on this — we'll have to bump your claims up.
SANDY	Let's think about your claims. What about subscriptions? Aren't you a member of the Marine Commando Club — Paddington?
Kenneth Horne	(*anxiously*) How do you know that?
SANDY	Seen you up there haven't we, Jule.
JULIAN	With that swarthy palone.
SANDY	Oh yes — her with the gold tooth and the plastic flower in her riah, and that's not all.
Kenneth Horne	If you're referring to Miss Fifi la Bootstrap — she's a talented cabaret artiste — I was helping her with her career.
SANDY	It's alright ducky. We've all got your number. What can we put her down as?
Kenneth Horne	A momentary lapse.
SANDY	No, I mean tax-wise heartface.
JULIAN	Now then, stop it you two. Did she buy you a drink, Mr Horne?
Kenneth Horne	Yes. Why?

JULIAN	Well we'll claim her as a foreign buyer.
SANDY	Now what about dependents. How many dependents have you got?
Kenneth Horne	None to speak of . . .
JULIAN	See if you only had some dependents we could really bump your claims up. We could claim for their clothing, holidays, allowances, cars. It really would make all the difference to your tax position.
SANDY	Still I think we can get round it. Just sign these forms.
Kenneth Horne	Alright. There. What are they exactly?
JULIAN	Adoption papers.
Kenneth Horne	Who have I adopted?
SANDY	Jule and me.
JULIAN	Daddy!

ORCHESTRA	**BRIEF LINK**
Kenneth Horne	I confidently expect that my tax worries are over. After all now I've got two 'omes to support. Now, what's the reverse of a bonne bouche, because that's what we've got now as I introduce Rambling Syd Rumpo.
RAMBLING SYD Kenneth Williams)	Hello me deario.
Kenneth Horne	Now what have you found in your ganderbag for us this week?
RAMBLING SYD	Well I was leafing through a book of eighteenth-century cheese sandwiches and I came across an old cordwangler's ditty. Now there's a lot of talk about cordwangling these days — but very few people know what it actually is — and those that practise it don't like to talk about it.
Kenneth Horne	I believe in the old days an apprentice was bound to a cordwangler for several years.
RAMBLING SYD	Yes, but they've stamped it out now — it ruined the circulation. Anyway the song tells of a cordwangler who gives his lady love several things to prove his devotion — and goes after this fashion . . .

GUITAR ACCOMPANIMENT

I gave my love a Bogle
that had no spring.
I gave my love a moulie
that didn't ring.
I gave my love a grunger
that had no spout.
I gave my love a nadger — without trying.

How can there be a Bogle
that has no spring.
How can there be a moulie
that doesn't ring.
How can there be a grunger
without a spout.
How can you give a nadger without trying.

A Bogle when it's wangled —
it has no spring.
A moulie when it's mangled —
it doesn't ring.
A grunger when it's broken —
it has no spout.
Your nadger when it's roasted
is most trying — ooooh!

(*applause*)

Kenneth Horne	Well that brings us to the end of the show, except for a police message Will Mr Grisley Larksbodice who left his home in Goatharbour Lane, Greenock at 9.30 am on the fourteenth of March 1741 please get in touch with his wife immediately, as his supper is getting cold. This, by the way, a repeat of a message broadcast earlier.
	Cheerio — see you next week.
	(*applause*)
ORCHESTRA	**'ROUND THE HORNE' PLAYOUT**

ROUND THE HORNE

3RD SERIES — PROGRAMME NO. 20
TRANSMISSION: Sunday 25th June 1967:
1.30-1.59 p.m. LIGHT PROGRAMME

Douglas Smith	And now the moment you've all been waiting for — the last programme in the current series of Round The Horne.
ORCHESTRA	**SIGNATURE TUNE**
OMNES	AD LIB 'SHAME' ETC.
Kenneth Horne	As it is the last programme of the series I would like to take this opportunity to acknowledge the sources of the material we have used. Thanks first to Tel Aviv Press Associates for permission to use extracts from their book A Hundred And One Things A Boy Can Do With A Smoked Herring. To Messrs Goosefit and Butterpant for passages from their book Up The Orinoco On A Liver Sausage. To the Posing Brief Collectors' Journal for permission to use poems from their Quiet Corner and to the over eighties Nudist Leap Frog team's quarterly satirical magazine, Private Thigh, for their article on 'The turnip — its place in nudism'. Our thanks too to the many people behind the scenes — To Jimmy Currie for his magic waterfall effect. To Jimmy Water for his magic curry effect . . . Cigarettes were by Cowlip and Pewterbland. Mr Williams was hatted by Thrupp, trousered by Cloot and booted by the Reverend Unseemly Kukpowder for taking advantage of his daughter. Mr Pertwee's clothes came from Gentlemen's Misfits as indeed did Mr Pertwee. Miss Marsden's foundation garments were kindly supplied by the Steel Company of Wales and Mr Hugh Paddick's wardrobe was by the Old Time Furnishing Boutique Limited. Mr Edwin Braden appears by permission of Rentawig. Alright, Smith — the podium is yours —
Douglas Smith	Thank you sir. Now it can be told — the story that the world has been waiting to hear. In recent weeks many top BBC executives have defected to commercial television — these defections were organised by a man who shall be nameless . . .
Kenneth Williams	David Paradine Nameless.
Hugh Paddick	Here then is a dramatic reconstruction of these events as we bring you — 'The Head of the BBC Who Came In From The Cold'.
ORCHESTRA	**DRAMATIC LINK**
GNOMEFUMBLER (Kenneth Horne)	My name is Ramsden Gnomefumbler. I'm Head of Security at the BBC Television Centre, or the free world as it's known. My code number is BBC 2 which means I'm licenced to lose money. One night I was on duty at the Great Shepherd's Bush Wall — the only thing that kept the free world from being overrun by the forces of David Paradine Nameless. Suddenly there was a movement in the darkness and I saw the tiny, almost human figure of Robin Day scaling the wall — I drew my Smith and Wesson Tin of Baked Beans with the silencer attached — and fired —
F/X	**GUNSHOT AND RICOCHET (GRAMS)**
ROBIN DAY (Bill Pertwee)	Alright — don't shoot — I'm coming down.
GNOMEFUMBLER	What are you doing?
ROBIN DAY	I was trying to defect over the wall.
GNOMEFUMBLER	It's a good trick if you can do it. Why do you want to leave the BBC? Aren't you happy here?

ROBIN DAY	It's not that — but I've been offered things — material things — a new spotted bow tie — a chair that swivels all the way round — diamante frames for my glasses.
GNOMEFUMBLER	Who's offered you these things?
ROBIN DAY	The Free Revolutionary Organisation for Stealing Talent.
GNOMEFUMBLER	The initials spelt out the dreaded word FROST, the name the BBC feared most — I called the guards and the unfortunate Day was hustled off to a place where no human being would see him again — Late Night Line Up. Then I hurried to report to my chief, the Controller of Programmes, Sir Todd Grunge.
F/X	**DOOR OPEN**
GNOMEFUMBLER	Excuse me sir —
SIR TODD GRUNGE	What is it, Gnomefumbler?
GNOMEFUMBLER	I've just caught Robin Day trying to escape.
GRUNGE	You brought him back?
GNOMEFUMBLER	Yes sir.
GRUNGE	Fool.
GNOMEFUMBLER	But things are looking serious sir.
GRUNGE	I know — In the last week we've lost most of our top men. Frank Muir — Doreen Stevens — Whicker.
GNOMEFUMBLER	I'd love to sir — but she wouldn't let me.
GRUNGE	We know the men behind it. There are three men in the consortium.
GNOMEFUMBLER	The way I heard it, it was three old ladies.
GRUNGE	Michael Peacock, Aidan Crawley and David Frost. Here are their photos. This one's Crawley, this one's pretty crawley too, and this one's right down creepy. They've done their fiendish work so well there's hardly anyone left — and not only executives, our stars are going as well. Twenty Four Hours is now twenty-four theirs — we've lost so many of our big names that our top show of the week is the news in Welsh.
GNOMEFUMBLER	How can I help sir?
GRUNGE	We want you to worm your way into the consortium and bring back Frank Muir. We don't think he wanted to go — we think he was drugged — judging by his appearances on Call My Bluff.
GNOMEFUMBLER	But won't they notice?
GRUNGE	They may. That's why we've got you this dummy.
GNOMEFUMBLER	What is it?
GRUNGE	It's an inflatable Frank Muir — made of rubber — you blow it up here.
GNOMEFUMBLER	My word — that's ingenious.
F/X	**BLOWING UP FRANK MUIR**
GNOMEFUMBLER	Good heavens — it's perfect down to the last simulated rubber pimple.

GRUNGE	Don't blow it up too much or it looks like Jimmy Edwards. On the oth hand, if you don't blow it up enough it looks like a baggy Jimmy Clitheroe. Your job is to substitute the replica and bring back the real Frank Muir — dead or alive — if you can tell the difference.
GNOMEFUMBLER	But how will I get into the FROST set-up?
GRUNGE	By posing as a refugee from the Television Centre looking for employment. Here is your disguise. Change of clothes so — some make ι — so. Just put on this wig — there — Jean Metcalfe to the life.
GNOMEFUMBLER	Do you think it'll fool them sir?
GRUNGE	It should do — but one word of warning, keep clear of Cliff Michelmo Now here are your accessories — a two-way mirror, a two-way radio and two-way family favourite —
GNOMEFUMBLER	Sir Todd gave me one of his icy stares — I slid down them and made n way to the FROST headquarters, an enormous limousine parked somewhere in Kensington. I knocked at the door. It was opened by th assistant head of FROST, the sinister Colonel George Postule.
COL. GEORGE POSTULE (Betty Marsden)	(gruff) What do you want?
GNOMEFUMBLER	My name is Jean Metcalfe. I want to defect to your organisation.
POSTULE	(gruff) You can't come in till you've been vetted.
GNOMEFUMBLER	The swine — he'd stoop to that would he.
POSTULE	Before you join us you must be brain washed. We don't allow anybody here with dirty minds.
GNOMEFUMBLER	Before I could protest I was roughly bundled into the five minute bra wash and fifteen Pakistanis swarmed all over me with damp shammy
Bill Pertwee	(Indian) There, all done — would you like your libido waxed? Or an freeze put in your id?
GNOMEFUMBLER	No thanks.
POSTULE	Come on Jean — it's time to meet him.
GNOMEFUMBLER	The Colonel pressed a button in his waistcoat and the flap of his hacki jacket slid back to reveal a secret passage — I followed him down it un we came to the inner sanctum. There, on an enormous gilt throne sat man they called David Paradine Nameless —
DAVID PARADINE NAMELESS (Kenneth Williams)	(snide) 'Ere, hello — Super to see you. So you're Jean Metcalfe. Sup welcome to the consortium. Let me show you round my organisation. here are my script writers.
F/X	**DOOR OPEN**
F/X	**BABBLE OF HUGE CROWD. CLANKING OF CHAINS**
Hugh Paddick	(exhausted) Champagne, champagne!
NAMELESS	Back, back you dogs. Back to your typewriters. You don't get your rati of champagne until you've written fifteen more pages of jokes about Harold Wilson and George Brown.

Hugh Paddick	(*exhausted*) I can't — I can't do another joke about George Brown. He's not funny — you can't make me. It's against the Geneva Convention.
NAMELESS	You'll do as you're told.
Hugh Paddick	(*exhausted*) But the conditions, they're inhuman — the overcrowding is terrible — we're working five hundred to a script — twenty men have to use the same joke — the ad libs are filthy. I want to go back — back to the BBC — back to writing 'I'm Sorry I'll Read That Again' where life was clean and decent and fine. I can't stand it here — I'm going to end it all.
NAMELESS	Quick stop him — He's got a double-edged reference.
Bill Pertwee	Drop it — Ah would you. Alright. I've got him sir. What shall I do with him? Shall I put him back to work?
NAMELESS	No, he's finished. He's no use to himself or anybody else — there's only one thing to do with him —
GNOMEFUMBLER	What's that?
NAMELESS	Sell him to Bob Monkhouse.
Hugh Paddick	(*exhausted*) No — no — etc. (*as he is led off*)
NAMELESS	You see how we operate Miss Metcalfe — just one big happy family.
GNOMEFUMBLER	You fiend, Nameless.
NAMELESS	This is only the beginning — one day I shall dominate the world. I shall be known and feared everywhere — I shall have power (*mad laugh*) power — I shall take over the universe!! (*pause*) (*sincerely*) But I hope I'll be able to retain my humility. Well Miss Metcalfe, what do you think?
GNOMEFUMBLER	I can no longer keep up my facade — I just felt the elastic go. I am not Jean Metcalfe. See I rip off my wig, I rip off my female attire — so. Now, do you recognise me?
NAMELESS	Twiggy!
GNOMEFUMBLER	No, not Twiggy. That's just a trick of the light. I am Ramsden Gnomefumbler of BBC security and this lemon meringue pie I'm holding is pointing straight at you. One move and I'll throw it.
NAMELESS	Quick — seize him.
ODD JOB (Hugh Paddick)	(*Robin — as with Batman*) I come to do your bidding oh mighty one.
NAMELESS	Seize the infidel, Odd Job.
ODD JOB	Yes master.
GNOMEFUMBLER	Odd Job?
NAMELESS	Yes, he only works part time. There are other reasons but this isn't the time or place . . . He's a dumb brute — but loyal.
GNOMEFUMBLER	The huge figure of Cyril Odd Job Bennett lumbered towards me. As he approached he took off his steel rimmed bowler hat — then his horn rimmed glasses, then his corrugated iron combs with the serrated edges — and with a cry of —

ODD JOB	Coo that's better!
GNOMEFUMBLER	— he leapt at me and we grappled.
	(*ad lib grunts*)
ODD JOB	Now with this hand I grab you here —
GNOMEFUMBLER	Groan.
ODD JOB	With this hand I grab you there —
GNOMEFUMBLER	Groan.
ODD JOB	And with this hand I — hold on, how did that hand get there?
GNOMEFUMBLER	It's mine.
ODD JOB	That's a relief. Now I hold you by the wrist so — then I hold you round the waist, so —
GNOMEFUMBLER	What happens now?
ODD JOB	We dance.
GRAMS	TANGO ('SPIDER OF THE NIGHT')
Kenneth Williams	Odd Job Bennett is wearing a décolleté boiler suit encrusted with diamante whelks which he's sewn on himself. Ramsden Gnomefumbler is wearing a daringly low-cut mohair vest with just a hint of mo at the vee. The card has slipped from Gnomefumbler's back but not to worry — we've all got their number — and with that I return you to the plot.
GNOMEFUMBLER	Things were going badly for me. Odd Job had me in a grip like a vice.
Kenneth Williams	What?
GNOMEFUMBLER	I said 'like a vice'.
Kenneth Williams	No thanks. I've got one. Pause for laugh and then does other line to clean up any misunderstanding: and I'm trying to give up smoking. (NAMELESS) Have you got him pinioned Odd Job?
ODD JOB	Yes, oh mighty one.
NAMELESS	Then throw him into the awful jaws of the Sacred Douglas Smith — resurrected from programme three by popular demand —
Douglas Smith	Snap snap —
	(*applause*)
Douglas Smith	Thank you fans. And now a day in the farmyard — why it's Nellie the sheep — Baa Baa —
Kenneth Williams	Alright — we've all heard it. Stop dragging your part out. (NAMELESS) Goodbye Gnomefumbler — prepare to meet your maker —
GNOMEFUMBLER	No — no!
Douglas Smith	Snap snap.

SNAP!

GRAMS	**DICK BARTON MUSIC**
Betty Marsden	Meanwhile in his office at the Television Centre, grizzled, lovely Huw Wheldon hears the cries for help on his secret two-way head. He leaps to his feet and screwing them on, he utters the mystic phrase that changes him from his almost impenetrable disguise as a dynamic TV executive to 'SuperHuw' — guardian of democracy.
Hugh Paddick	(*shouts*) Tam ratings kazam!
Bill Pertwee	Clad now in gold lamé tights worn under his swimming trunks, and a PVC cape and mask, SuperHuw leaps out of the window and in an instant breaks his leg.
Betty Marsden	But six months later, at the consortium . . .
GNOMEFUMBLER	No — no.
Douglas Smith	Snap — snap.
F/X	**WHOOSH**
Kenneth Williams	What is it? Is it a bird? Is it a plane? . . .
Hugh Paddick	(*Welsh*) No, it is I SuperHuw, look you — with a leek in my hat and another one in my head, come to do battle for democracy, freedom and the black and white minstrels.
GNOMEFUMBLER	Have you come to save me?
Hugh Paddick	No.
GNOMEFUMBLER	Have you come to rescue Frank Muir?
Hugh Paddick	No.
GNOMEFUMBLER	Then why have you come?
Hugh Paddick	Well, I just wondered, Mr Nameless, sir — have you got a job for me?
ORCHESTRA	**PLAY OFF**
Kenneth Horne	I ought to point out that the foregoing was entirely fictitious and bears no relation to the real events (*Horne laugh*). And now for our wonderful singing group — the Fraser Hayes Four — without whom the show would be a lot shorter. Here then, more in sorrow than in tune — The Fraser Hayes Four.
SER HAYES FOUR CHESTRA	**MUSIC BREAK**
	(*applause*)
Douglas Smith	And now, the Round The Horne Colour Supplement.
Kenneth Horne	First a word from Daphne Whitethigh.
DAPHNE WHITETHIGH (Betty Marsden)	Ipecacuana.
Kenneth Horne	And thank you for that word, Daphne Whitethigh — now it's time to meet TV Sunday night personality, Seamus Android.

SEAMUS ANDROID	Well, Hello — Alright — Well now — ha ha — well as it's the last time, I'd like to be the first to say hello to a young lady who can hold her own — as far as I'm concerned — till the cows come home. What's that? Oh —they have — well, far be it from me, although I can reach it if I stretch, so let's put them together warmly and join with me in a heartfelt — cos I know how I feel and don't need any advice from you — so with that — Goodnight.
Kenneth Horne	Thank you Seamus Android — every Sunday night I feel that nothing would make me happier than to sit at your feet — and set fire to your trousers. And now the Colour Supplement turns its attention to the Englishman and his body.
DENTURES (Hugh Paddick)	So you want a new body do you?
Bill Pertwee	Yes, that's right. Your advertisement says a new body in seven days or your money refunded.
DENTURES	That's absolutely so — we guarantee a body that you'll really be proud of. Just sign this chit.
Bill Pertwee	How much is it?
DENTURES	Ten pounds.
Bill Pertwee	Very reasonable — who do I make it payable to?
DENTURES	Just make it out to Messrs Burke and Hare. Thank you, Dr Knox.
ORCHESTRA	**BRIEF LINK**
Kenneth Horne	Nowadays the magazines are full of advertisements offering to develop all or part of you by post. You know the sort of thing — "A new bust by mail". Parcel post, I assume — but there's no doubt about it, the physical culture business is expanding all the time.
GRUNTFUTTOCK (Kenneth Williams)	Excuse me, are you Charles Collosus the body builder?
COLLOSUS (Hugh Paddick)	Yes. What can I do for you Mr — er —
GRUNTFUTTOCK	Gruntfuttock. J. Peasemold Gruntfuttock. I'm told you can build me a body that'll be the envy of my neighbours.
COLLOSUS	(dubiously) Yes.
GRUNTFUTTOCK	You won't believe this but once I was a seven stone weakling.
COLLOSUS	What are you now?
GRUNTFUTTOCK	Six stone twelve. That's why I come to you. Last summer at the beach i was just like in your advertisements. Bullies kicked sand in my face.
COLLOSUS	Why did they do that?
GRUNTFUTTOCK	Because I was peering through a knothole in the bathing hut. When I go to the beach I dare not take my raincoat off.

COLLOSUS   Why?

GRUNTFUTTOCK   I have no bathing trunks. When I read your advertisement it gave me new hope. I cut this photo out the paper — here look — I want a body like this.

COLLOSUS   But this is a photograph of Ursula Andress.

GRUNTFUTTOCK   Yes I know — good isn't she.

COLLOSUS   But I can't possibly develop your body like this. The best I can do is give you a body like mine.

GRUNTFUTTOCK   It's not for me. It's for the wife. She's already got a body like yours.

ORCHESTRA   **SHORT LINK**

Kenneth Horne	Physical culture is inseparable from the sun and the open air and that probably explains the current craze for nudism — and it's nice to know that these dedicated nudists can, even among the hurly burly of nut cutlets and volley ball, find time for a little old-fashioned romance.
GRAMS	**'ISN'T IT ROMANTIC'**
BINKIE HUCKABACK (Hugh Paddick)	Fiona —
CELIA MOLESTRANGLER (Betty Marsden)	Charles —you recognised me.
BINKIE	Yes. I never forget a face. How lovely to see you again.
CELIA	And you Charles.
BINKIE	How do I look? Do I look different?
CELIA	You've aged, Charles, and yet you've still got that boyish twinkle.
BINKIE	Funny our marriage never worked out.
CELIA	Funny though that we never got a divorce.
BINKIE	Perhaps we half knew, half hoped, half thought, half dreamed, half guessed — that somehow, somewhere, sometime, some way we'd —
CELIA	We'd what Charles?
BINKIE	I'm afraid I've forgotten.

CELIA	Do you remember when we last met? At the nudists' masked ball.
BINKIE	And we didn't recognise each other until midnight when we took our masks off.
CELIA	It was a fancy dress ball.
BINKIE	I wore only an eye patch and went as Lord Nelson. At least I *think* it was Lord Nelson.
CELIA	Well you weren't Lady Hamilton.
BINKIE	And now we meet again. Naked as nature intended.
CELIA	Yes. How people stare though —
BINKIE	Let them stare — haven't they ever seen two nudists before —
CELIA	Not like this — not in the grill room of the Ritz.
ORCHESTRA	**LINK**
Kenneth Horne	We stay in the open air, which is just as well, when you consider that our next guest is Rambling Syd Rumpo.
RAMBLING SYD RUMPO (Kenneth Williams)	Hello me deario — crying gander my lummocks — who'll traddle my turve
Kenneth Horne	Any volunteers? Now Rambling Syd, what are you going to burst forth with this week?
RAMBLING SYD	Tis the tale of a young recruit who has been spurndled in love by a taddlesome maid and his possets are full sore and his cordwangle hangs heavy — so he rushes off to Brighton to join the army but alas he fails the medical on account of flat scropers, so he sings after this fashion —

To the tune of 'Girl I Left Behind Me'

GUITAR ACCOMPANIMENT

My wogglers both have lost their bloom
No bogling do I fancy —
My artifacts are bended low
Since parting with my Nancy.
I'll seek no more to grunge my hod,
My grummetts they do bind me.
Oh how I long to toast my splod
With the girl I left behind me.

Oh ne'er shall I forget the day
We plighted our cordwangle —
And how could I forget the way
Her bosky moulies dangle.
But now I'm bent for Brighton Camp
And no-one there shall find me.
Beneath the pier I'll lunge my groats —
To the girl I left behind me.

Kenneth Horne	Thank you Rambling Syd. That brought tears to my wogglers and raise goosepimples on my artifacts. Now, I must confess that I too have succumbed to the craze for body building — and so when I saw an advertisement in my copy of the Medical Cummerbund Exchange and Mart — I buy it for the 'What's wrong with this picture' competition — anyway, when I saw this advertisement which read 'Do you want bulging biceps and massive lallies? Apply to Body Bona — inventors of the lightning method', I hurried over to their address in Chelsea straightaway.
F/X	DOOR OPEN
Kenneth Horne	Hello — is there anybody there?
JULIAN (Hugh Paddick)	Oh hello — I'm Julian and this is my friend, Sandy.
SANDY (Kenneth Williams)	We are your actual physical culturists Bona Bods. We've got cups for i
JULIAN	I was Mr Marine Commando Club in 1966 and Sand was placed in the Mr Universe of Balls Pond Road contest.
SANDY	We have hundreds of unsolicited testimonials haven't we Jule?
JULIAN	Oh yes — Nante solicited — they just come pouring in.
Kenneth Horne	Well you certainly are a remarkable pair of specimens.
SANDY	Thanks — take your shirt off Jule. Show Mr Horne your rippling physique —
JULIAN	Don't like to.
SANDY	This is no time for modesty. It's his modesty that lets him down. He'd b Mr Universe only he was too embarrassed to take his pully off.
JULIAN	Oh alright —
SANDY	There, look Mr Horne. Vada that great butch lucoddy — ripple your muscles Jule. He does it to music Mr Horne. Like that chap on Opportuni Knocks.
JULIAN	Well put the record player on.
SANDY	Right — go.
GRAMS	MUSCLE RIPPLING MUSIC AS USED BY MAN ON 'OPPORTUNITY KNOCKS'
SANDY	Go it Jule — shake 'em about. Look at his metatarsals going like the clappers — and look at his triceps going — it's as if they've got a life of their own. Now your lallies Jule — quiver your lallies for the gentleman He's got thews on him like a Percheron. Now, all together — fantabulosa
GRAMS	MUSIC OUT
JULIAN	There, what do you think?
Kenneth Horne	Very impressive.
JULIAN	Course it is thanks to Mother Nature I have got independent suspension
SANDY	Independent control — Jule.

JULIAN	Oh yes.
SANDY	Course it didn't come overnight — he had to work at it.
JULIAN	Yes. I used to be a puny little omi. I had lallies like a flamingo — and narrow shoulders.
SANDY	Yes. He had to cross his braces to keep his trousers up.
JULIAN	And a little pale eek, and lifeless riah.
SANDY	He was like a wallflower Mr Horne.
Kenneth Horne	That wasn't the flower that came to mind.
SANDY	A wallflower he was. Now he's a hardy annual aren't you Jule?
JULIAN	Thanks to Sand and his method. He showed me his dynamic tension and overnight I become the great butch omi you vada now.
Kenneth Horne	What is your method?
SANDY	A rigid diet — and it's got to be rigid. No backsliding. Then there's your exercises and, of course, weightlifting. Show him your two-handed snatch Jule. Go on — look Mr Horne — see that barbell over there — Jule is going to lift that above his head.
JULIAN	Just putting some resin on my hands. Right — here goes (*breathes deeply then grunts with effort*).
SANDY	(*ad lib encouragements*) There — he's got it up past his knees — look — look at the way he's holding that barbell over his head.
Kenneth Horne	His eek's showing the strain.
SANDY	There the barbell's above his head.
JULIAN	(*with great effort*) I can't hold it any longer. What shall I do with it?
SANDY	Ring it.
JULIAN	Oh alright.
F/X	**TINY HAND BELL TINKLING**
SANDY	We always have drinkies about this time.
F/X	**DOOR OPENS AND CLUMPING FOOTSTEPS COMING IN**
GORDON (Bill Pertwee)	You rang, master Jule?
JULIAN	Yes Gordon — three pints of crème de menthe and put a head on mine.
GORDON	Righto.
F/X	**CLUMPING FOOTSTEPS OFF. DOOR SLAM**
SANDY	That's Gordon. He helps us out — he's a sort of masseur. He'll give you a good pummelling.
JULIAN	As soon as look at you.
SANDY	He's a rough diamond Mr Horne, but underneath — deep down inside . . .

JULIAN	He's absolute rubbish.
SANDY	Well — he's not *my* friend. You brought him here.
JULIAN	He was down on his luck. I'm like that. I can't turn a stranger away.
SANDY	Yes — and you won't find anyone stranger than Gordon. Still he's a certified psychopath.
Kenneth Horne	Don't you mean osteopath?
SANDY	We know Gordon better than you do. Now, about our course — you going to enrol?
Kenneth Horne	What actually does it entail?
JULIAN	Well briefly — every morning you have a cross country troll — then you have a work out on the bars —
SANDY	Then you have to do fifty press ups and skip for an hour.
JULIAN	Then you have your sauna bath — where you wallop yourself with twigs.
SANDY	You'll enjoy that. Then there's weightlifting, physical jerks, your all round P.T., cycle twenty-four miles — then breakfast.
Kenneth Horne	It sounds pretty spartan.
SANDY	It is. Our seven day method is a way of life. Of course you'll have to give up things.
Kenneth Horne	What things?
JULIAN	Well, smoking, drinking, eating solid foods and palones.
SANDY	Yes, you'll have to give 'em all up.
Kenneth Horne	Why?
SANDY	Seven days with us and you won't have the strength for them.
ORCHESTRA	**PLAY OFF**
Kenneth Horne	I took the course and last week I entered for the Mr South Kensington competition — I was highly commended for my abdomen — got an honourable mention for my triceps — and I would have won — but I fell down on my metatarsals. Well, that brings us to the end of our series, and there only remains one thing to do — but I'll just have to wait till we're off the air. Cheerio — see you soon.
ORCHESTRA	**PLAY OFF**

Douglas Smith	That was the last in the present series of Round The Horne —
ORCHESTRA	**MUSIC UNDER FOR —**
BINKIE	So it's goodbye is it Fiona?
CELIA	Not goodbye Charles.
BINKIE	Well, au revoir then.
CELIA	Not au revoir.
BINKIE	Auf wiedersehen?
CELIA	Not auf wiedersehen.
BINKIE	Then what the hell is it — we've got to finish somehow . . . .
	(*applause*)
GRUNTFUTTOCK	On behalf of my good lady Slagheap and myself, I would like to say — alright, I'm coming constable.
	(*applause*)
SEAMUS ANDROID	And this is Seamus Android saying hello — alright — goodbye.
F/X	**GONG**
LOTUS BLOSSOM	What is it oh mighty mandarin?
CHOU EN GINSBERG	Ah Lotus Blossom my little lychee nut — I just want to say goodbye, darling.
LOTUS BLOSSOM	Ta ta cock.
	(*applause*)
RAMBLING SYD	Ta ta my dearios — and remember keep your moulies up and smile through your possetts — cause I know that one day we'll whirdle each other again.
Betty Marsden	Many many times.
JULIAN	So this is it Sand —
SANDY	Don't cry Jule — be brave — mince tall.
	(*applause*)
Douglas Smith	And this is Douglas Smith saying in the voices of the characters I've played in the past weeks — Chug chug, moo moo, baa baa, phut phut, snap snap, splosh.
Kenneth Horne	And to think he gets paid for that. Cheerio.
	(*applause*)
ORCHESTRA	**'ROUND THE HORNE' PLAYOUT**

19 6.67.

Dear Barry & Martie
Barrie & Marty

I would find it quite impossible
to write entirely different "thank you"
letters to you two miracle men, so
you can assume that this is
"To Took, copy to Feldman" and
"To Feldman, copy to Took"

Honestly I don't know how
you've done it, but you have! And
what's more every programme has
been a riot.

What interests me is that on the
very rare occasions when we suspected
that a particular show wasn't going
to come over quite as well as usual,
whether for scriptual, castual

or audiencual reasons, the results always showed how wrong we were.

It's been a smashing series — easily the best, & must have broken all records. But I doubt not that those records will be broken again when we all get together for the next group of epics.

I have already turned down a suggestion that the new series should be entitled: "A Song, a smile and Edna Purbright", because I feel that it sounds too much like "Panorama".

May the team of Took & Feldman (copy to Feldman & Took) long flourish.

What's more it's been wonderful fun to do — and if that isn't a compliment to script-writers I don't know what is. Have you ever tried working to a script in which you don't believe?

Thanks again!
& all the best

POSTSCRIPT

Kenneth Horne died on the 14th February 1969 and with him Round The Horne died too.

It does seem absurb to say that Round The Horne was the happiest of shows — but it was. I hope this book has helped you to share some of that happiness.

BARRY TOOK

Printed by C. J. Mason & Sons Ltd.,
Bristol BS13 7TP.